The Children's Cookbook

A Beginner's Guide to Cooking

P.O. Box 77, Nashville, Tennessee 37202
Library of Congress Cataloging in Publication Data
Main entry under title:
The Children's cookbook.
Includes index.
SUMMARY: A beginner's cookbook with cooking definitions, helpful hints, and recipes for snacks, parties, picnics, entire meals, and microwave ovens.
1. Cookery—Juvenile literature. [1. Cookery]
I. Favorite Recipes Press/Nashville EMS.
TX652.5.C46 641.5'123 80-13492
ISBN 0-87197-130-5

Dear Young Cooks:

Everyone loves to eat! Now you can learn to cook your favorite foods, too. This cookbook has simple recipes—easy enough for even Mom to make. Fun and good food go together, but when you make it yourself it's twice as much fun.

Using this cookbook you can help Mom out by making food for snacks, parties, picnics or even a whole meal. You can also use your new cooking skills to welcome the new kid on the block, cheer a sick friend or even fix Dad's lunch for work.

You'll find recipes for fixing a snack for you and your friends or an entire meal for family or company. Included are helpful hints, cooking definitions, even special recipes for microwave.

The wonderful smells from the kitchen will have your family ready to "Come and get it." You'll be proud when everyone asks for "Seconds, please!"

Sincerely,

Mary Jane Blount

Table of Contents

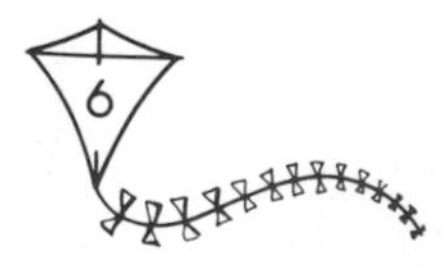

Things To Remember

1. **ALWAYS** check with your mother before you start to cook—she's had lots of experience. Ask her to show you how to use the stove and small appliances.

2. Before you start—read the recipe all the way through. Make sure you have everything you need, including ingredients and the correct utensils.

3. Wash your hands and put on an apron or an old shirt—cooking can be messy.

4. Use exactly the amount called for in the recipe. Use level measurements, rather than heaped up.

5. When using a knife or vegetable peeler, **ALWAYS** cut away from yourself. Use a chopping board so you won't scratch the counter top. Never leave knives where younger children can reach them.

6. Be very careful with anything that might be hot. Always use a potholder to hold the handle of the pot while stirring. Use a potholder to pull out the oven rack. Use a potholder to take things from the oven. Never set anything hot on a counter top.

7. Stir a hot mixture on the stove with a wooden spoon or a metal spoon with a wooden or plastic handle. Never leave a spoon in the pan.

8. Turn the handles of saucepans inward on the stove, so no one will bump the handle while walking by.

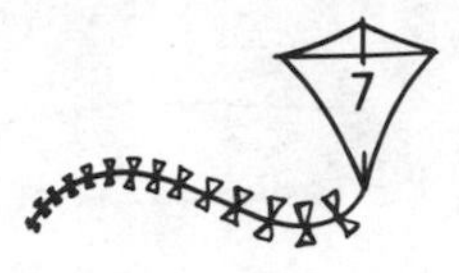

9. Remember **NEVER** put any metal or aluminum foil in your microwave oven.

10. **ALWAYS** plug in electrical cords with dry hands. Keep the cords out of water and away from mixer, blender and stove top.

11. Use a clock with large numbers if you do not have a timer.

12. Use a fork for stirring dry ingredients and use a spoon for stirring liquids.

13. To grease a baking dish, use a paper towel dipped in butter, margarine or cooking oil.

14. Use paper towels to wipe up spills right away!

15. Tap an egg against the sharp edge of the bowl just enough to crack the shell. Hold it over the bowl and with your fingers, open the crack to let the whole egg drop into the bowl.

16. Hold onions under cold water while you peel them so you won't "cry".

17. When you have finished cooking, make sure that the oven, burners and lights of the stove are turned off.

18. Keep your kitchen as neat and clean as possible while you cook. Learning to cook includes learning to clean up.

8/Utensils

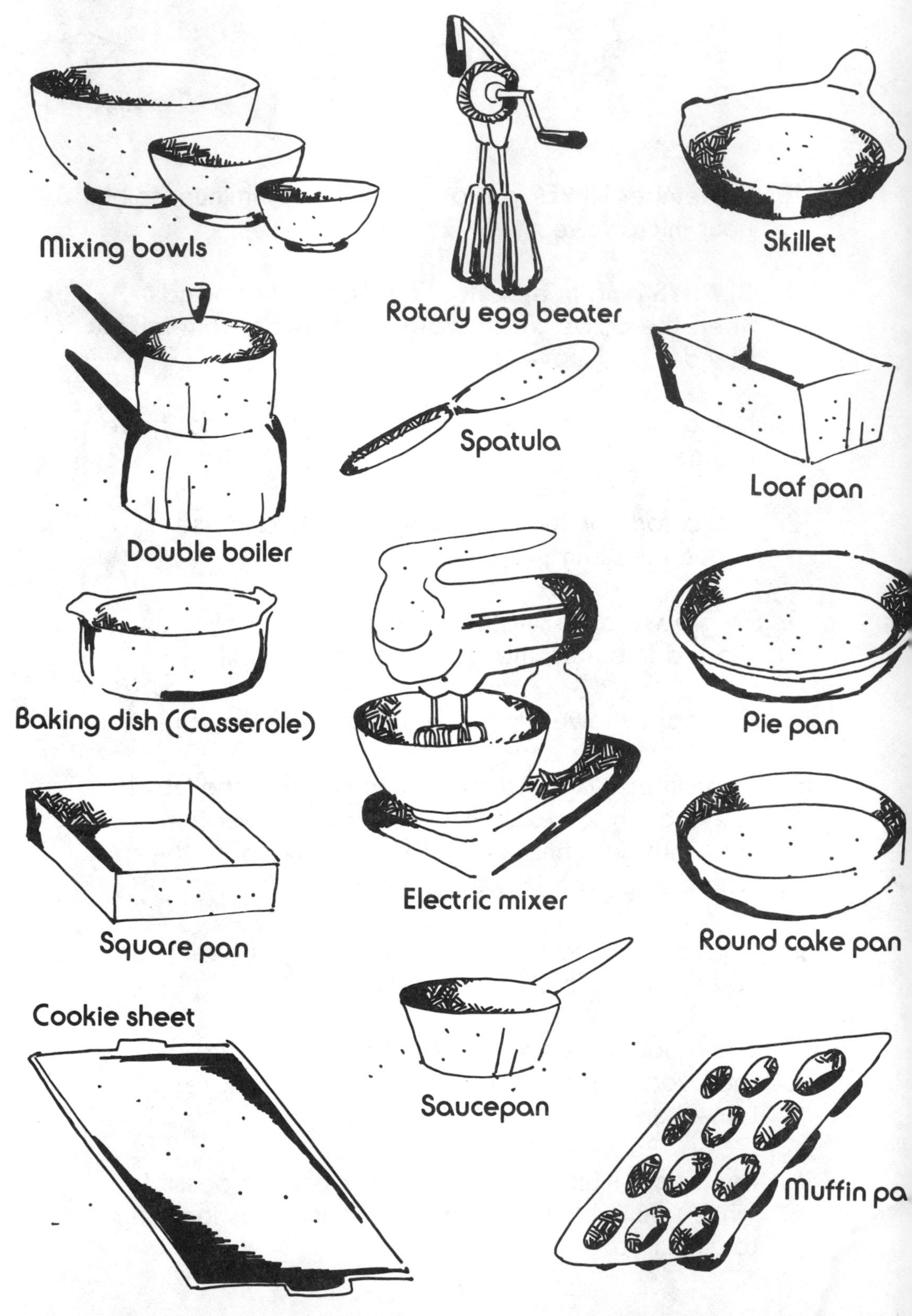
Mixing bowls
Rotary egg beater
Skillet
Double boiler
Spatula
Loaf pan
Baking dish (Casserole)
Electric mixer
Pie pan
Square pan
Round cake pan
Cookie sheet
Saucepan
Muffin pa

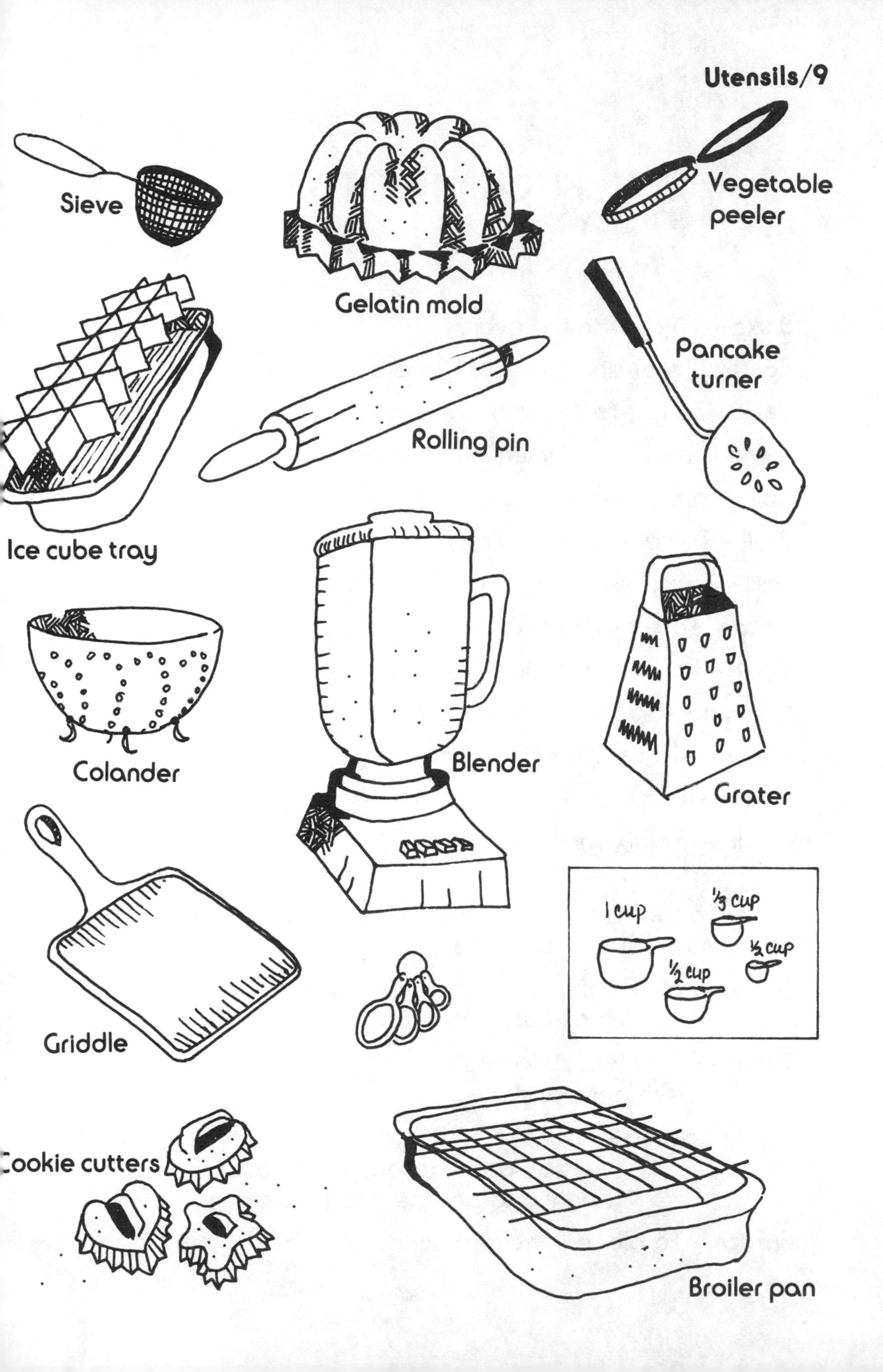
Sieve
Gelatin mold
Vegetable peeler
Ice cube tray
Rolling pin
Pancake turner
Colander
Blender
Grater
Griddle
1 cup
1/3 cup
1/4 cup
1/2 cup
Cookie cutters
Broiler pan

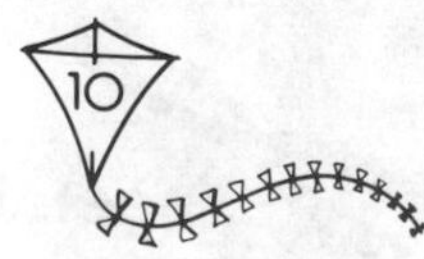

KNOW WHAT IT MEANS . . .

Bake - To cook in the oven.

Baste - To brush liquid over food as it cooks.

Beat - To mix fast with beater or spoon.

Blend - To mix ingredients until smooth.

Boil - To cook until liquid bubbles.

Broil - To cook in oven directly under heat of broiler.

Chill - To place in refrigerator to lower temperature of food.

Chop - To cut into small pieces.

Coat - To cover a food completely, usually with flour.

Combine - To mix the ingredients.

Cream - To beat until soft and fluffy.

Cube - To cut food into small pieces with 6 sides.

Cut in - To mix shortening with dry ingredients, using two knives.

Dice - To cut food into very small pieces, approximately the same size and shape.

Dot - To put small pieces of one food on top of another food, such as butter on top of casserole.

Drain - Pour off liquid or let it run off through the holes in a sieve or colander.

Firmly packed - To make sure ingredients, such as brown sugar, are packed into measuring cup tightly to get the correct amount.

Freeze - To place in freezer until set.

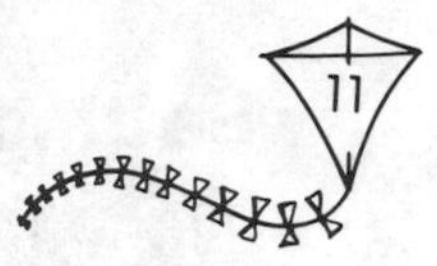

Fry - To cook in hot shortening.

Grate - To rub on a food grater to break the food into fine pieces.

Grease - To rub the surface of the utensil with shortening or butter to prevent sticking.

Knead - To fold and press dough with heel of hand.

Melt - To heat until solid becomes liquid.

Mince - To cut into tiny pieces.

Mix - To stir ingredients together.

Pare or peel - To remove outer skin.

Pinch - The very small amount of an ingredient that can be held between the finger and thumb, for example, pinch of salt.

Shred - To cut into thin strips with a shredder.

Shortening - Fats such as butter, margarine, lard and vegetable oil and solid.

Sift - To shake dry ingredients (flour, baking powder) through a sieve or sifter.

Simmer - To cook over low heat until food barely bubbles.

Soften - To take food from refrigerator or freezer to let it get soft.

Stir - To mix slowly with spoon or fork.

Whip - To beat very fast.

Setting The Table

1. Cup and Saucer	7. Napkin
2. Teaspoon	8. Salad Plate
3. Knife	9. Bread and Butter Plate
4. Dinner Plate	10. Butter Knife
5. Fork	11. Glass
6. Salad Fork	

The setting above may show more plates and silver than you need. If so, just remove the pieces you do not need.

If you are serving, always serve from the left and remove dishes from the right.

Snacks

Cheese Delight Sandwich

1 slice bread
Mayonnaise
1 slice cheese
1 slice tomato
1 slice onion
1 strip bacon

Spread............bread with mayonnaise.
Add.................in layers, cheese, tomato and onion slice.
Cut..................bacon strip in half and place on onion slice.
Place...............on broiler pan. Turn oven setting to Broil.
Broil................until cheese begins to melt.

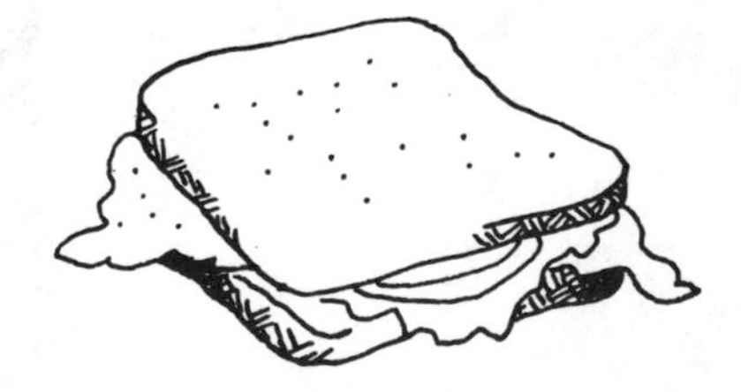

Cheese Puff Sandwiches

8 slices bread
4 slices Cheddar cheese
2 eggs
1 cup milk
½ teaspoon salt
Pinch of pepper
¼ teaspoon dry mustard

Preheat............oven to 350 degrees.
Arrange............4 bread slices in large greased baking dish. Cover each with a cheese slice. Place remaining bread slices on cheese slices.
Beat................eggs until frothy.
Add..................milk, salt, pepper and dry mustard; mix well. Pour over sandwiches.
Refrigerate........until milk is absorbed into bread.
Bake.................at 350 degrees for 30 minutes.
Yield................4 servings.

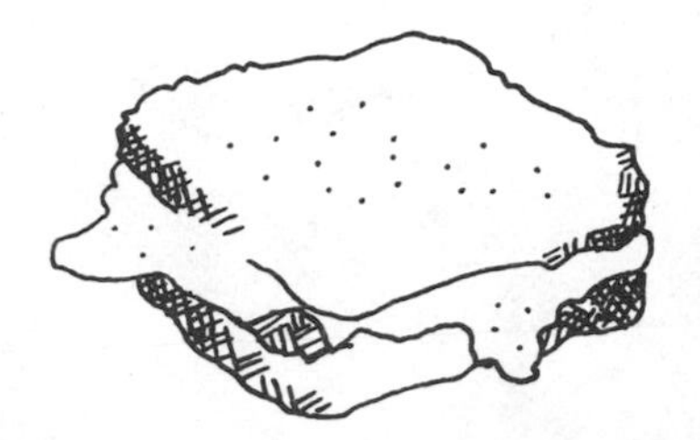

Dogs In A Blanket

10 wieners
Cheese
1 10-count can biscuits

Preheat............oven to 375 degrees.
Split..................each wiener but not completely through.
Slice..................cheese to fit into slit of wiener.
Flatten.............each biscuit; place 1 wiener on flattened biscuit. Roll biscuit around wiener; secure biscuit around wiener with toothpick.
Place................on cookie sheet.
Bake.................at 375 degrees for 10 minutes or until biscuits are browned.
Yield................10 servings.

Dotted Soup

3 wieners
1 can tomato soup
1 soup can milk
Parmesan cheese

Cut .... wieners crosswise into thin circles.
Pour .... soup into saucepan. Slowly add 1 soup can milk, stirring until mixture is smooth.
Cook .... over Medium heat; stir until mixture is hot. DO NOT BOIL.
Add .... wiener slices to soup.
Cook .... over Medium heat for 5 minutes more. DO NOT BOIL.
Pour .... soup into bowls.
Sprinkle .... with Parmesan cheese.

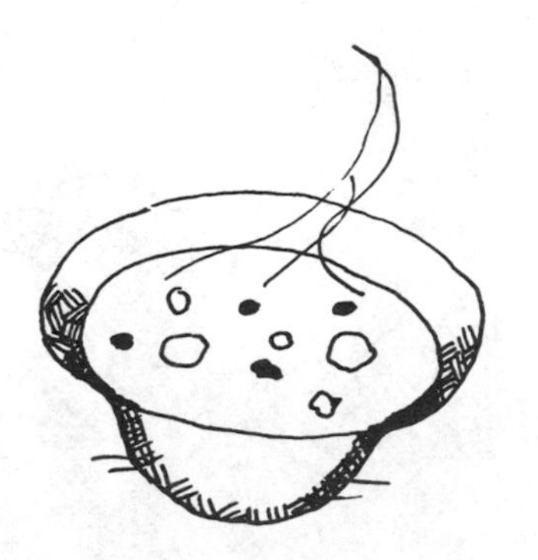

Fancy Franks

6 buns, halved and buttered lightly
6 wieners, split almost through lengthwise
1 onion, chopped
6 slices Velveeta cheese
Catsup

Arrange............bun halves on broiler pan.
Place...............wieners, spread open, on buns.
Sprinkle............with onion.
Cover................with cheese.
Pour.................catsup over cheese.
Broil.................until cheese melts. Serve hot.
Yield................6 servings.

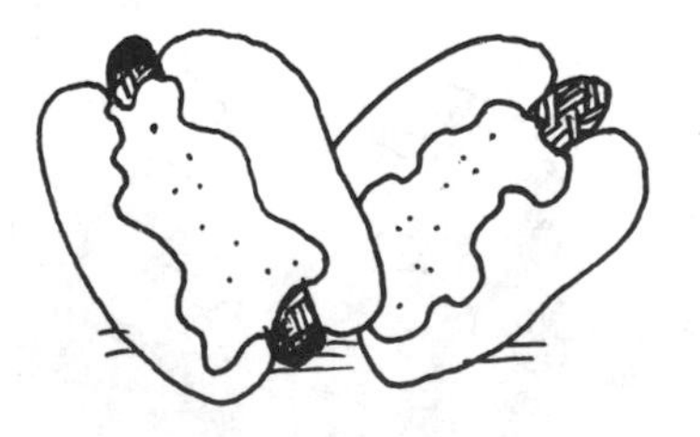

Fried Cheese Sandwich

2 slices bread
Mayonnaise
1 slice Cheddar cheese
Butter

Spread............. 1 slice bread with mayonnaise; top with cheese.
Butter................ remaining bread slice; place, unbuttered-side down, on cheese.
Melt.................. pat of butter in skillet. Place sandwich, unbuttered-side down, in skillet.
Cook................. until brown and cheese melts.
Turn.................. sandwich over; brown.
Yield................ 1 serving.

Italian Grilled Cheese

8 slices Italian bread
4 slices mozzarella cheese
8 thin slices salami
Oregano
Butter

Top.................. each of 4 bread slices with 1 cheese slice and 2 salami slices.
Sprinkle............ each with dash of oregano; top with bread slice.
Butter............... both sides of sandwich generously.
Place............... on hot griddle; brown on both sides.
Yield................ 4 servings.

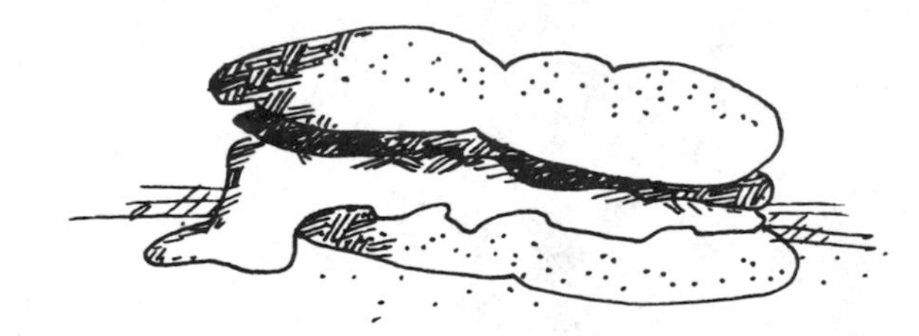

Maple Milk Shake

1 pint chocolate ice cream, softened
1 quart cold milk
½ cup maple syrup

Place................ ice cream, milk and syrup in mixer bowl.
Beat................. with an electric mixer.
Pour................. into glasses. Serve cold.

Pizza Hot Dogs

4 hot dog buns
4 wieners
12 slices mozzarella cheese
Pizza sauce
Parmesan cheese, grated

Split..................hot dog buns and wieners lengthwise.
Place................layer of cheese on buns.
Add..................wiener slices to each bun.
Top..................with pizza sauce.
Sprinkle............with Parmesan cheese.
Place................on broiler pan.
Broil.................until brown and bubbly.

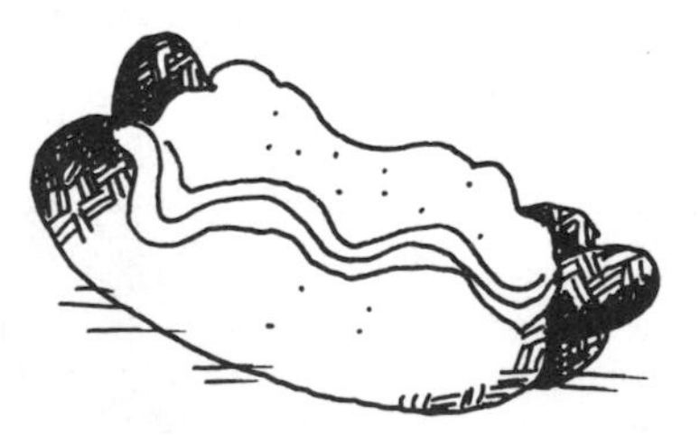

Popsicles

1 large package Jell-O
1½ cups hot water
1 package Kool-Aid, same flavor as Jell-O
1 cup sugar
2½ cups cold water

Dissolve............Jello-O in 1½ cups hot water.
Add.................Kool-Aid, sugar and 2½ cups cold water.
Pour................into Tupperware molds or other molds used for popsicles. Freeze.

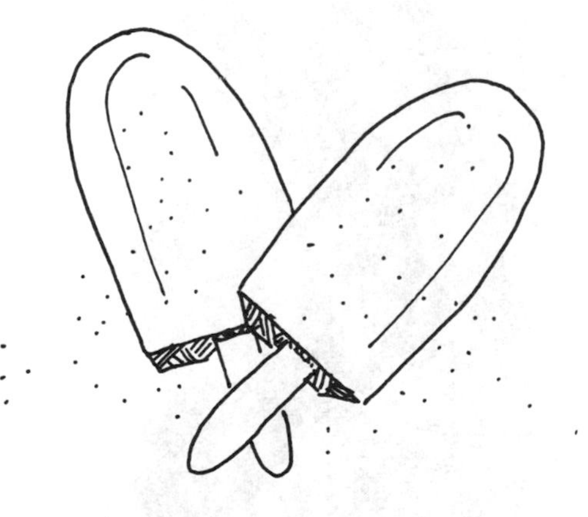

Saucy Grilled Sandwich

1 6-ounce jar peanut butter
½ cup applesauce
4 slices frozen French toast
Margarine, softened

Combine...........peanut butter and applesauce in small mixer bowl; mix well.
Spread.............peanut butter mixture on 2 slices of toast.
Top..................with remaining toast slices.
Spread.............margarine on both sides of sandwiches.
Place...............on griddle or in skillet. Brown on each side.

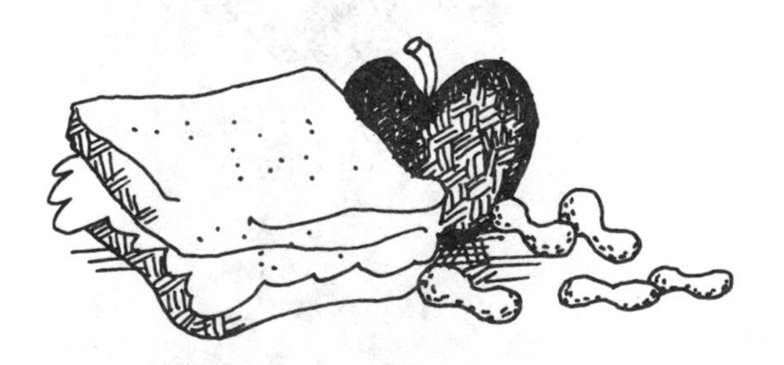

Super Peanut Butter Sandwich

5 tablespoons peanut butter
3 tablespoons cream cheese, softened
2 tablespoons honey
4 slices bread

Combine........... peanut butter, cream cheese and honey; mix well.
Spread............. on bread slices.
Yield................ 4 servings.

Tunaburgers

1 7-ounce can tuna
1 cup chopped celery
½ cup American cheese, cut in pieces
¼ cup mayonnaise
1 small onion, chopped
Salt and pepper to taste
8 buns

Preheat .... oven to 350 degrees.
Mix .... tuna, celery, cheese, mayonnaise, onion, salt and pepper.
Fill .... buns with tuna mixture.
Wrap .... in foil.
Bake .... at 350 degrees for 15 to 20 minutes.
Yield .... 8 servings.

Meats

Chicken and Rice

2 cups minute rice
1 can mushroom soup
1 can celery soup
½ cup milk
1 frying chicken, cut up
1 package dry onion soup mix

Preheat............oven to 325 degrees.
Grease.............8 x 13-inch baking dish.
Sprinkle............rice over bottom of greased baking dish.
Pour................mushroom soup, celery soup and milk in saucepan. Heat on Medium heat until soup mixture is heated through. DO NOT BOIL. Pour over rice; stir.
Lay..................pieces of chicken over rice mixture, skin side up.
Sprinkle............dry onion soup mix over chicken pieces. Cover baking dish tightly with aluminum foil.
Bake................at 325 degrees for 2 hours and 15 minutes.

Chinese Tuna Casserole

1 6½-ounce can tuna
1 cup chopped celery
½ cup chopped onions
1 can mushroom soup
1 cup water
1 small can Chinese noodles
½ cup chopped cashews

Preheat............oven to 325 degrees.
Combine...........tuna, celery, onions, soup, water and Chinese noodles in large mixing bowl; mix well.
Pour.................into baking dish.
Top...................with cashews.
Bake.................at 325 degrees for 40 minutes.

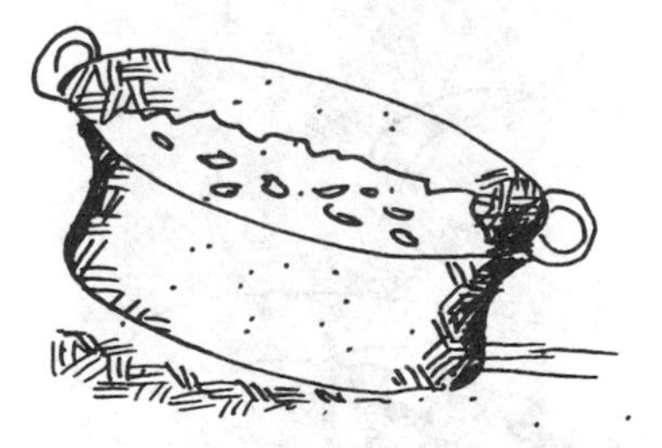

Easy Chili

1 pound ground beef
1 cup chopped onion
2 15½-ounce cans kidney beans
1 can tomato soup
½ cup water
2 tablespoons chili powder
½ teaspoon salt
Dash of pepper

Place............... ground beef and onion in large heavy saucepan.
Cook................ over Medium heat until ground beef is browned.
Pour................ off grease.
Add................. beans, tomato soup, water, chili powder, salt and pepper; cover.
Simmer............ for 1 hour.

Glazed Chicken

¼ cup shortening
¼ cup catsup
¼ cup lemon juice
2 tablespoons Worcestershire sauce
6 chicken pieces
¼ teaspoon salt
Pinch of pepper

Preheat............oven to 350 degrees.
Combine...........shortening, catsup, lemon juice and Worcestershire sauce in saucepan. Bring to a boil; remove from heat.
Arrange............chicken pieces in baking dish.
Sprinkle............with salt and pepper.
Pour.................sauce over chicken pieces.
Bake.................at 350 degrees for 45 minutes. Turn chicken pieces several times during baking.

Ham and Cheese Casserole

8 slices bread, crusts removed
4 slices ham
4 slices American cheese
4 eggs
½ cup milk
1 teaspoon prepared mustard
¼ teaspoon salt
Pinch of pepper
Paprika

Grease .... 2-quart baking dish.
Cover .... bottom of greased baking dish with 4 bread slices.
Place .... 1 ham slice and 1 cheese slice over each bread slice.
Top .... each with bread slice.
Mix .... eggs, milk, mustard, salt and pepper in mixing bowl.
Pour .... over bread.
Place .... in refrigerator for 4 hours.
Bake .... at 300 degrees for 30 minutes.
Sprinkle .... with paprika.

Hamburger Pie

2 pounds hamburger
Salt and pepper to taste
2 teaspoons chopped onion
2 packages frozen French fries
1 can cream of chicken soup
1 can cream of mushroom soup

Preheat............oven to 350 degrees.
Pat..................hamburger into bottom of cake pan. Sprinkle salt, pepper and onion over hamburger.
Arrange............frozen French fries in layer over hamburger.
Spread.............soups over French fries.
Bake................at 350 degrees for 1 hour.
Cut..................into squares to serve.
Yield...............8 servings.

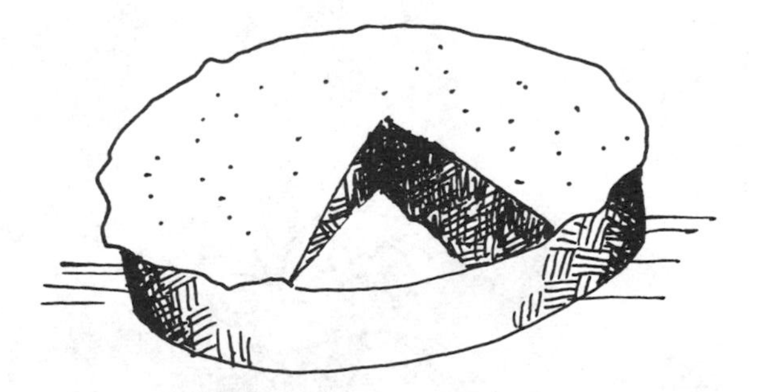

Hamburger-Tater Tot Casserole

1 pound hamburger
¼ cup chopped onion
1 package frozen Tater Tots
1 can cream of mushroom soup
¾ cup milk

Preheat............oven to 350 degrees.
Place...............hamburger and onion in large skillet. Stir hamburger with fork to break up large pieces. Cook over Medium heat until hamburger is browned; drain.
Place...............hamburger mixture in baking dish.
Add..................Tater Tots; mix well.
Combine...........soup and milk in mixing bowl; stir well.
Pour................soup mixture over hamburger mixture; stir well.
Bake................at 350 degrees for 30 minutes.

SLUMBER
PARTY !
12

Individual Pizzas

¼ pound hamburger
¾ cup tomato sauce
½ teaspoon oregano
¼ teaspoon salt
Pinch of garlic salt
1 can refrigerator biscuits
¾ cup grated cheese

Preheat............oven to 450 degrees.
Place...............hamburger in skillet. Stir hamburger with a fork to break up large pieces. Cook on Medium heat until hamburger is browned; drain.
Add.................tomato sauce, oregano, salt and garlic salt.
Pat..................out each biscuit on cookie sheet to form pizza crust.
Spread.............each biscuit with hamburger mixture.
Sprinkle............with grated cheese.
Bake.................at 450 degrees for 10 minutes.
Yield................10 servings.

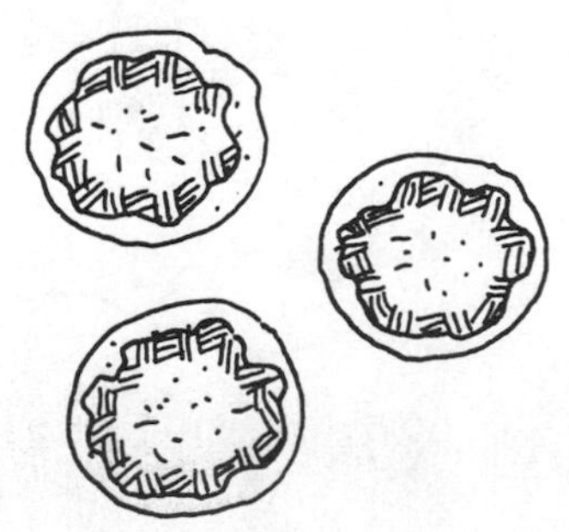

Jumbo Burgers

2 pounds ground beef
1 cup grated Cheddar cheese
¾ cup chopped onion

Mix..................all ingredients in large mixing bowl.
Roll..................into large patties, using hands.
Place...............patties on broiler pan. Turn oven setting to Broil.
Broil.................5 minutes. Remove from oven. Turn patties over using spatula. Return to oven.
Broil.................5 minutes longer.
Serve...............on large buns.
Yield................8 patties.

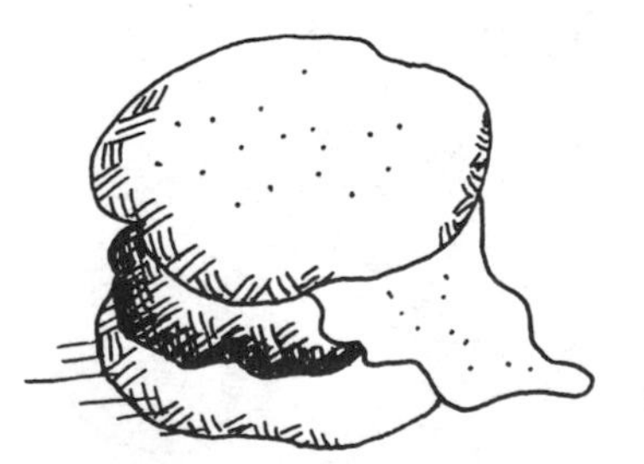

Meat Loaf

1 pound ground beef
⅔ cup evaporated milk
1 envelope dry onion soup mix

Preheat............oven to 350 degrees.
Mix..................ground beef, evaporated milk and onion soup mix in large mixing bowl.
Place...............ground beef mixture in shallow baking pan; shape into a loaf.
Bake.................at 350 degrees for 1 hour.
Yield................4 servings.

Microwave Golden Chicken

1 3-pound frying chicken, cut up
½ cup chopped celery
1 teaspoon salt
1 can golden mushroom soup

NEVER .... PUT METAL OR ALUMINUM FOIL IN THE MICROWAVE OVEN.

Arrange .... chicken, skin side up, in 2-quart glass baking dish.
Sprinkle .... with celery and salt.
Spoon .... soup over chicken. Cover with glass lid or plastic wrap.
Microwave .... on High for 30 minutes or until chicken is done.

Microwave Ham Roll-Ups

15 frozen Tater Tots
4 slices Swiss cheese
4 slices boiled ham
½ cup sour cream

NEVER..............PUT METAL OR ALUMINUM FOIL IN THE MICROWAVE OVEN.

Place...............Tater Tots in microwave oven on paper plate or towel.
Microwave........on High for 2 minutes or until thawed.
Place...............1 cheese slice on each ham slice. Spread each cheese slice with small amount of sour cream. Place 3 Tater Tots inside each ham-cheese slice; roll-up, fastening with a toothpick. Place on serving platter.
Microwave........on High for 2½ minutes or until hot.

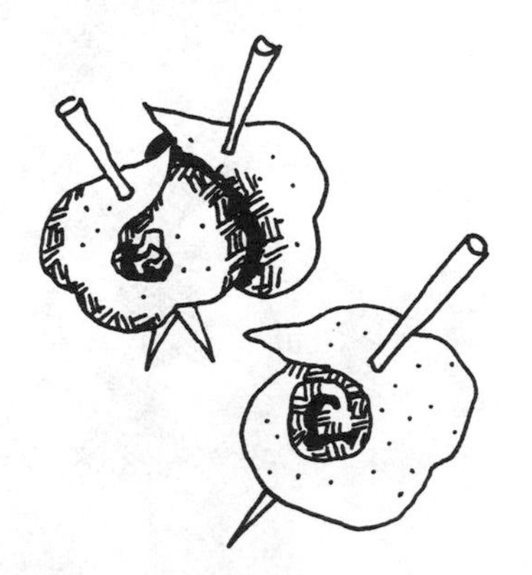

Microwave Hamburgers

1 pound hamburger
1 teaspoon salt
¼ teaspoon pepper

NEVER.............. PUT METAL OR ALUMINUM FOIL IN THE MICROWAVE OVEN.

Mix.................. hamburger meat, salt and pepper in large mixing bowl.
Shape.............. into 4 or 5 patties, using hands.
Place............... patties on 9-inch glass pie plate, dinner plate or platter without silver or metal trim.
Microwave........ on High for 3 minutes. Turn once. Microwave on High 3 minutes longer. Drain on paper towel.

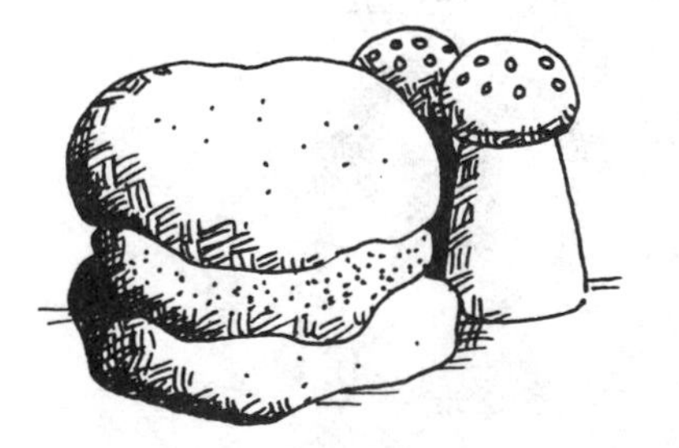

Muffin Meat Loaf

1 egg
½ cup milk
¾ cup oats
1 pound ground beef
3 tablespoons chopped onion
1 teaspoon salt
½ cup grated cheese

Preheat............oven to 350 degrees.
Grease.............cups in muffin pan.
Combine...........all ingredients; mix well.
Spoon...............mixture into greased muffin cups.
Bake................at 350 degrees for 1 hour.
Cool.................slightly before removing from muffin cups.

Pork Chop Bake

8 pork chops
1 teaspoon salt
8 slices onion
8 slices lemon
½ cup (firmly packed) brown sugar
¾ cup catsup

Preheat............oven to 350 degrees.
Place...............pork chops in large baking dish. Sprinkle with salt.
Top..................each pork chop with onion slice and lemon slice.
Mix..................brown sugar and catsup in small mixing bowl. Pour over pork chops. Cover.
Bake................at 350 degrees for 1 hour. Uncover.
Bake................at 350 degrees for 15 minutes longer.
Yield................8 servings.

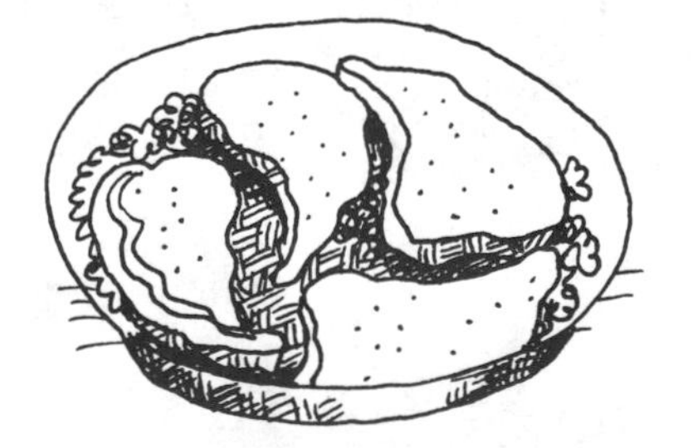

Salmon Patties

1 16-ounce can pink salmon
1 egg
⅓ cup chopped onion
½ cup flour
1½ teaspoons baking powder
1½ cups shortening

Drain................salmon, keeping 2 tablespoons of the liquid.
Mix...................salmon, egg and onion in mixing bowl until mixture is sticky.
Stir..................in flour.
Add..................baking powder to the 2 tablespoons of reserved liquid. Stir into salmon mixture.
Form.................into small patties, using hands.
Place................shortening in large skillet. Fry patties in shortening over Medium heat for 5 minutes. Turn patties once while frying. Place patties on several layers of paper towel to drain.
Yield................4-6 servings.

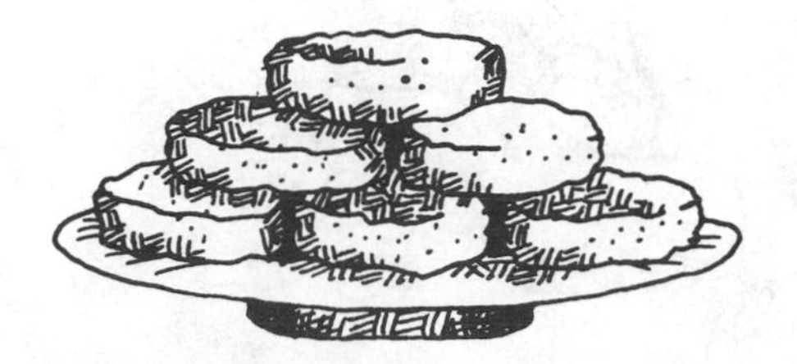

Smothered Pork Chops

4 thick pork chops
½ cup uncooked rice
1 medium onion
Salt
Pepper
1 lemon
1 can cream of mushroom soup

Preheat............oven to 325 degrees.
Trim..................fat from pork chops.
Place................pork chops in skillet over Low heat. Brown on both sides.
Pour.................rice into large baking dish; place pork chops over rice.
Cut...................onion into 4 slices; place 1 slice on each pork chop.
Sprinkle............with small amount of salt and pepper.
Cut...................lemon into 4 slices; place on onion slices.
Pour.................soup over pork chops. Cover.
Bake.................at 325 degrees for 1 hour.

Salads

Candlelight Salad

1 lettuce leaf
1 canned pineapple slice
1 small banana
1 maraschino cherry

Rinse................and drain lettuce leaf. Place on salad plate.
Place...............pineapple slice on lettuce leaf.
Cut..................banana flat on bottom to stand straight. Stand banana upright in pineapple hole.
Place...............cherry on top of banana to make the flame, using a toothpick to keep it in place.

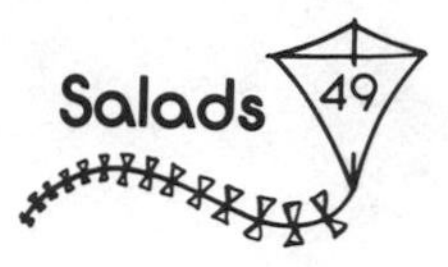

Five-Cup Salad

1 cup mandarin oranges
1 cup pineapple tidbits
1 cup coconut
1 cup miniature marshmallows
1 cup sour cream

Drain................oranges and pineapple.
Combine...........all ingredients in bowl.
Chill.................to serve.

French Dressing

1 cup catsup
1 cup vegetable oil
Juice of 1 lemon
½ cup white vinegar
½ cup sugar
1 small onion, grated
½ teaspoon salt

Place............... all ingredients in 1-quart jar. Cover tightly.
Shake............... jar vigorously to blend ingredients.
Refrigerate........ until serving time.

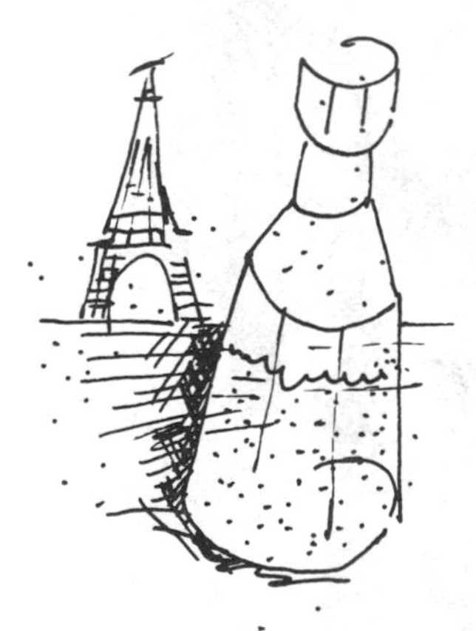

Frozen Cranberry Salad

1 1-pound can cranberry sauce
½ pint sour cream
1 7-ounce can crushed pineapple, drained

Combine............cranberry sauce and sour cream in mixing bowl.
Stir....................in pineapple.
Pour..................into ice trays without sections to freeze.
Serve................on lettuce.
Yield.................6 servings.

Fruit Salad

1 large can fruit cocktail, drained
2 bananas, sliced
1 cup sweetened flaked coconut

Mix..................all ingredients in mixing bowl.
Chill.................to serve.
Yield................6 servings.

Green Grape Salad

¼ cup mayonnaise
1 3-ounce package cream cheese, softened
Pinch of garlic salt
1 pound seedless green grapes

Combine........... mayonnaise and cream cheese; beat until smooth.
Add.................. garlic salt; beat again.
Add.................. grapes; stir until grapes are coated.
Chill................. until serving time.
Yield................ 4-6 servings.

Italian Dressing

½ cup (firmly packed) brown sugar
½ cup vinegar
½ cup catsup
½ cup salad oil
1 small onion, grated
Pinch of garlic powder
Pinch of dry mustard

Combine...........all ingredients in 1-quart jar. Cover tightly.
Shake...............jar vigorously to blend ingredients.

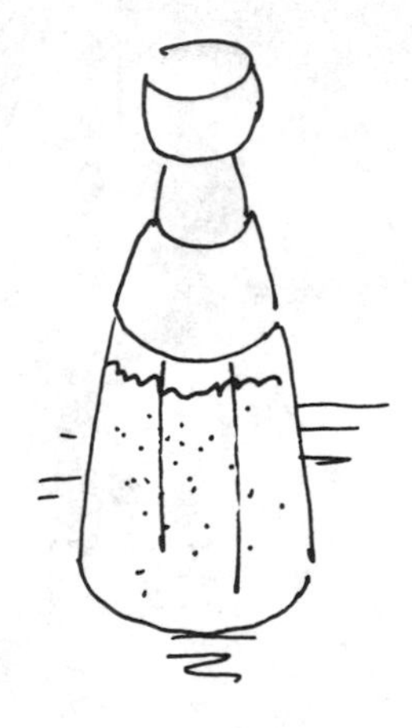

Raggedy Ann Salad

Body................Canned peach half
Arms and Legs....Small celery sticks
Head...............½ hard-cooked egg
Eyes, Nose.........Raisins
Buttons, Shoes....Raisins
Mouth..............Piece of a cherry or cinnamon candy
Hair.................Grated yellow cheese
Skirt.................Ruffled lettuce leaf

Red Applesauce Salad

1 No. 303 can applesauce
1 3-ounce package cherry Jell-O
1 6-ounce bottle 7-Up

Place............... applesauce in small saucepan; heat over Medium heat until bubbly hot.
Add.................. Jell-O; stir until Jell-O is dissolved. Cool.
Stir................... in 7-Up; mix well.
Pour................. into mold. Chill until set.
Yield................ 8-10 servings.

Tomato Flower

Lettuce
4 tomatoes
Cottage cheese
Paprika
French dressing

Rinse .... and drain lettuce.
Cut .... away core of tomato to hollow out. Cut each tomato into 8 wedges; do not cut all the way through. Place on lettuce leaf.
Fill .... tomato with cottage cheese.
Sprinkle .... with paprika.
Pour .... French dressing over top.

Tossed Green Salad

½ head lettuce
2 medium tomatoes
½ green pepper
2 carrots
½ medium onion
5 radishes

Rinse................and drain lettuce. Cut or tear into small pieces. Place in large salad bowl.
Cut..................tomatoes into small pieces. Add to lettuce.
Chop................green pepper into tiny pieces. Add to salad. Be careful not to get any seeds in the salad.
Scrape.............carrots with vegetable scraper. Cut off tops. Slice into thin slices. Add to salad.
Remove...........outer skin of onion. Chop into small pieces. Add to salad.
Cut..................tops from radishes. Cut each radish into 4 pieces. Add to salad.
Toss.................all ingredients, using a fork or spoon.
Pour................favorite dressing over all just before serving.

Vegetables

Asparagus Bake

1 can asparagus
3 slices American cheese
1 can mushroom soup

Preheat............oven to 350 degrees.
Drain................asparagus. Place asparagus in baking dish.
Break...............cheese into small pieces; add to asparagus.
Pour................soup over asparagus mixture.
Bake................at 350 degrees for 30 minutes.

Baked Pork and Bean Casserole

2 No. 303 cans pork and beans
1/3 cup (firmly packed) brown sugar
1 small onion, finely chopped
1/4 cup catsup
5 slices bacon

Preheat............oven to 350 degrees.
Pour................pork and beans into 1 1/2-quart casserole.
Add.................brown sugar, onion and catsup; mix well.
Top..................with bacon slices.
Bake................at 350 degrees for 1 hour.
Yield...............6 servings.

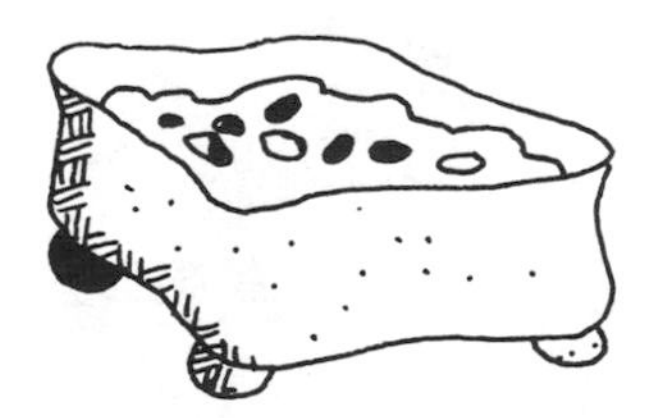

Baked Potatoes

1 potato per person
Shortening
Margarine

Preheat............oven to 425 degrees.
Wash................potatoes; scrub well. Dry on paper towel. Prick potato skins with fork.
Rub..................each potato well with about 1 teaspoon shortening.
Wrap................each potato in aluminum foil.
Bake................at 425 degrees for 1 hour. Unwrap; split potato—not all the way through.
Fill...................split with margarine.

Candied Carrots

¼ cup margarine
¼ cup jellied cranberry sauce
2 tablespoons sugar
½ teaspoon salt
4 cups canned sliced carrots

Preheat............oven to 350 degrees.
Combine...........margarine, cranberry sauce, sugar and salt in skillet; simmer on Low heat until cranberry sauce melts, stirring often.
Drain................carrots. Add carrots to cranberry mixture, stirring well.
Place...............in baking dish.
Bake................at 350 degrees for 10 minutes.

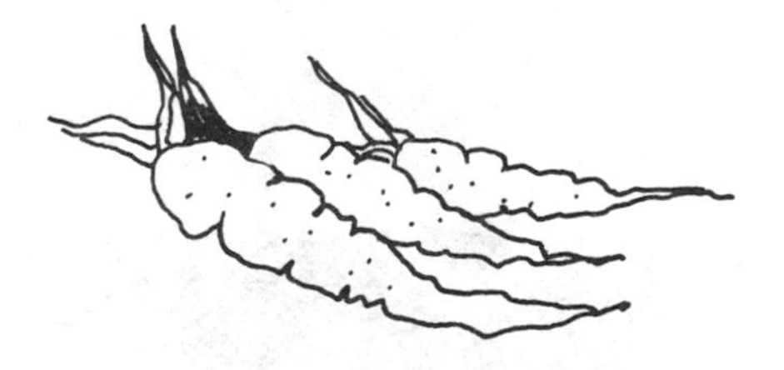

Confetti Corn

2 eggs
3 tablespoons margarine
4 cups canned corn
1 small jar chopped pimento
1 teaspoon salt
¼ teaspoon pepper
1 can onion rings

Preheat............oven to 350 degrees.
Grease.............1½-quart baking dish.
Break...............eggs into mixing bowl; beat well.
Heat................margarine in small saucepan over Low heat until melted.
Combine...........eggs, margarine, corn, pimento, salt and pepper in greased baking dish. Mix well.
Top..................corn mixture with onion rings.
Bake................at 350 degrees for 35 minutes.

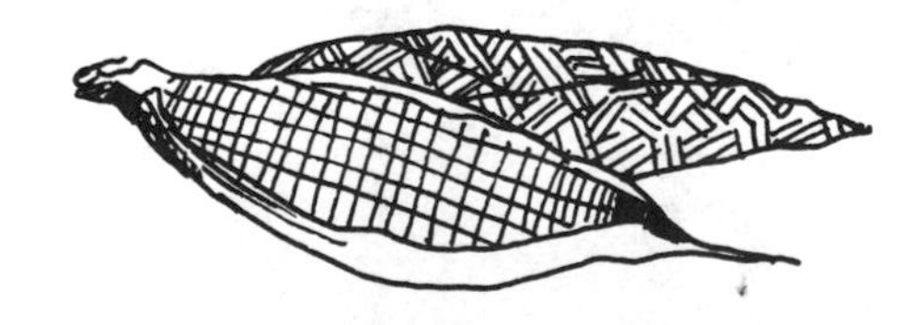

Creamed Broccoli

1 10-ounce package frozen broccoli
½ cup cubed cheese
1 can cream of mushroom soup

Preheat............oven to 350 degrees.
Grease.............1-quart baking dish.
Place...............frozen broccoli in greased baking dish.
Add.................cheese cubes.
Spoon...............on soup; cover.
Bake................at 350 degrees for 1 hour.
Yield...............4-6 servings.

Creamy Corn

¼ cup milk
1 3-ounce package cream cheese
1 tablespoon margarine
½ teaspoon salt
Pinch of pepper
3 cups whole kernel corn

Combine........... milk, cream cheese, margarine, salt and pepper in large saucepan.
Cook................ over Low heat, stirring all the time, until blended.
Drain................ corn well. Stir into cream cheese mixture, heating through.

Delicious Green Beans

2 cans green beans
1 can cream of celery soup

Preheat............oven to 425 degrees.
Drain................liquid from green beans; reserving ½ cup liquid.
Mix..................liquid with soup.
Arrange............green beans in baking dish.
Pour................soup mixture over beans; cover.
Bake................at 425 degrees for 45 minutes.
Yield................6-8 servings.

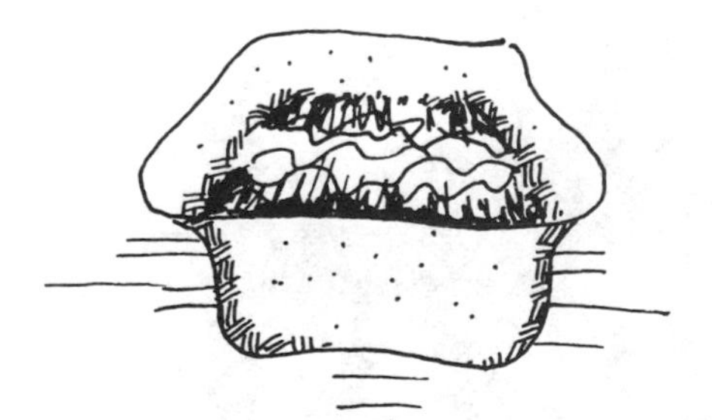

Golden-Glazed Carrots

1 pound carrots
2 tablespoons cooking oil
¼ cup water
2 tablespoons brown sugar
¼ teaspoon salt

Scrape.............. carrots with vegetable peeler. Slice into small pieces.
Pour................ cooking oil in saucepan.
Add................. carrots; cook over Medium heat until lightly browned.
Combine.......... water, brown sugar and salt. Pour over carrots; cover.
Cook................ over Low heat for 15 minutes.
Yield............... 4 servings.

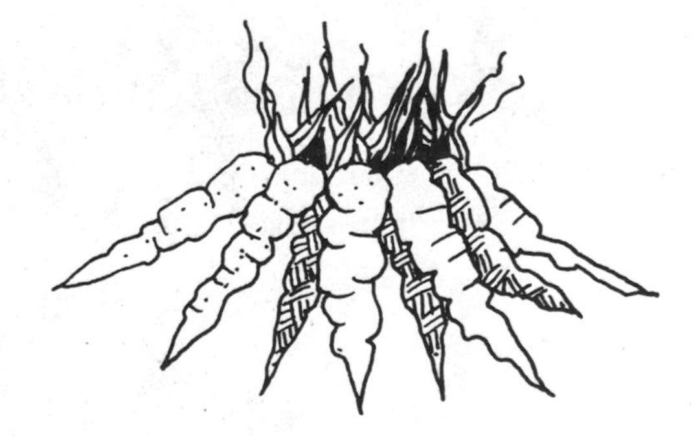

Honey-Butter Peas

1 package frozen green peas
¼ cup honey
¼ cup margarine

Prepare............peas according to package directions; drain.
Combine...........honey and margarine in small mixer bowl; beat until fluffy.
Pour................over peas. Serve immediately.

Microwave Glazed Sweet Potatoes

4 medium sweet potatoes
½ cup (firmly packed) brown sugar
¼ cup margarine

NEVER.............. PUT METAL OR ALUMINUM FOIL IN THE MICROWAVE OVEN.

Pierce.............. sweet potatoes with a fork. Place in microwave oven.
Microwave........ on High for 10 minutes or until tender.
Peel................. and slice into 1½-quart glass baking dish.
Sprinkle............ potato slices with brown sugar. Dot with margarine. Cover with glass lid or plastic wrap.
Microwave........ on High for 4 minutes; stir.
Microwave........ on High for 3 minutes longer. Let stand, covered, for 3 minutes before serving.

Microwave Honeyed Onions

8 medium whole onions, peeled
2 tablespoons margarine
½ cup honey

NEVER............... PUT METAL OR ALUMINUM FOIL IN THE MICROWAVE OVEN.

Place............... onions in 1-quart glass baking dish. Cover with glass lid or plastic wrap.
Microwave........ on High for 8 minutes; drain.
Stir.................. in margarine and honey; cover.
Microwave........ on High for 3 minutes longer. Let stand, covered, 3 minutes before serving.

Oven French Fries

4 medium potatoes, peeled
1 tablespoon corn oil
Salt to taste

Preheat............oven to 425 degrees.
Cut..................potatoes into ½-inch strips.
Pour................oil into baking pan. Add layer of potatoes, stirring to coat potatoes with oil.
Bake................at 425 degrees for 30 minutes; turn potatoes.
Bake................at 425 degrees for 10 minutes longer.
Sprinkle...........with salt.
Yield................4 servings.

Sweet and Sour Cabbage

2 cups chopped cabbage
1 tablespoon margarine
½ teaspoon caraway seed
½ teaspoon salt
1 tablespoon flour
1 cup water
1 tablespoon vinegar
2 teaspoons sugar

Combine............ cabbage, margarine, caraway seed, salt, flour and water in large saucepan. Cover.
Simmer............. on Low heat for 10 to 15 minutes.
Add.................. vinegar and sugar; mix lightly.

Vegetable Casserole

1 10-ounce package frozen peas
1 10-ounce package frozen carrots
1 No. 303 can small onions, drained
2 10½-ounce cans cream of celery soup
½ soup can milk

Preheat............oven to 350 degrees.
Combine...........all ingredients in 1½-quart casserole.
Bake................at 350 degrees for 1 hour.
Yield................6-8 servings.

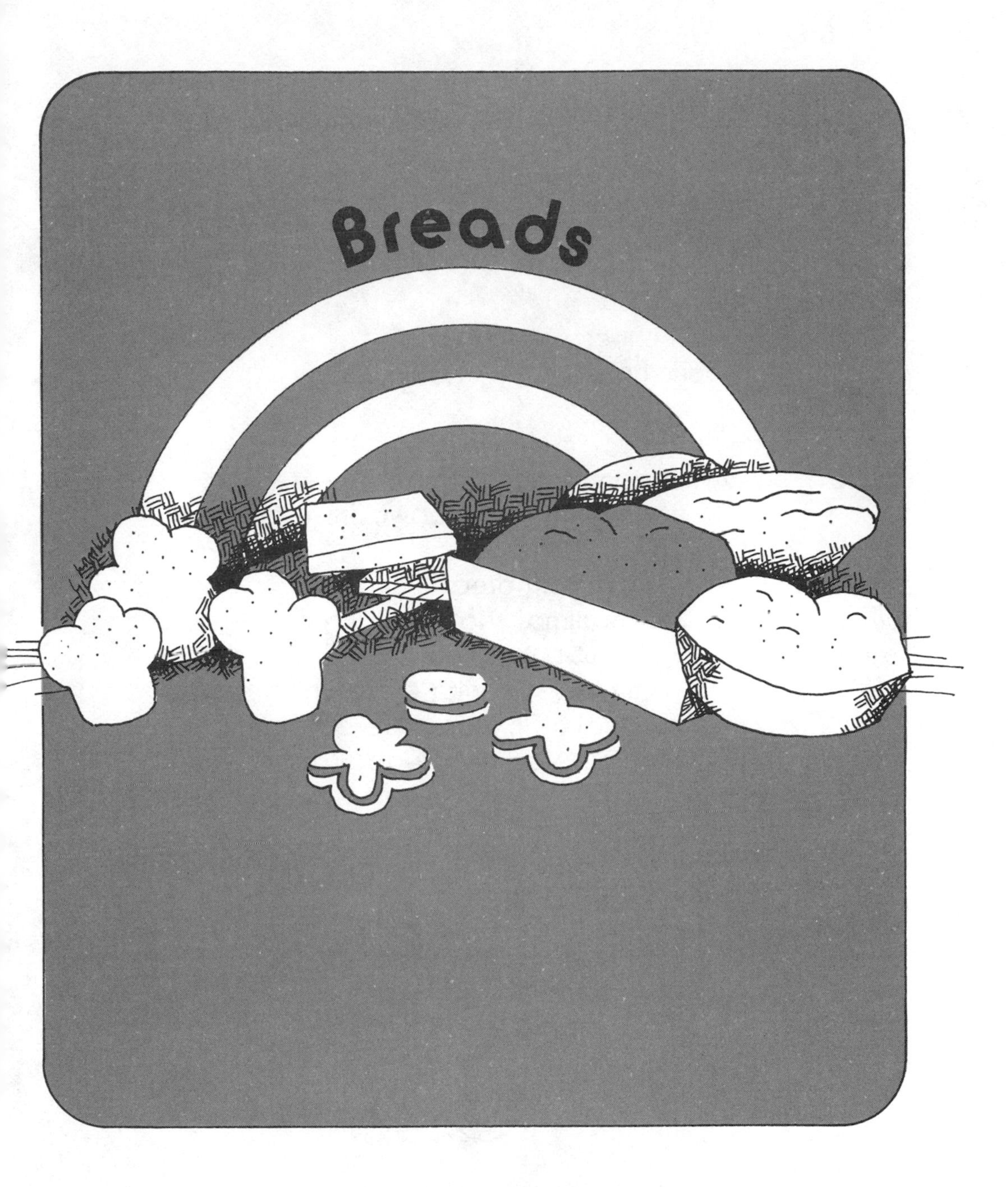
Breads

Animals

⅓ cup peanut butter
¼ cup cream cheese, softened
2 tablespoons honey
Bread

Place............... peanut butter, cream cheese and honey in mixing bowl. Stir until well blended.
Trim................. crusts from bread.
Cut.................. into animal shapes, using cookie cutters.
Spread............ peanut butter on half the bread animals. Top with a matching bread animal . May be covered and refrigerated until ready to serve.

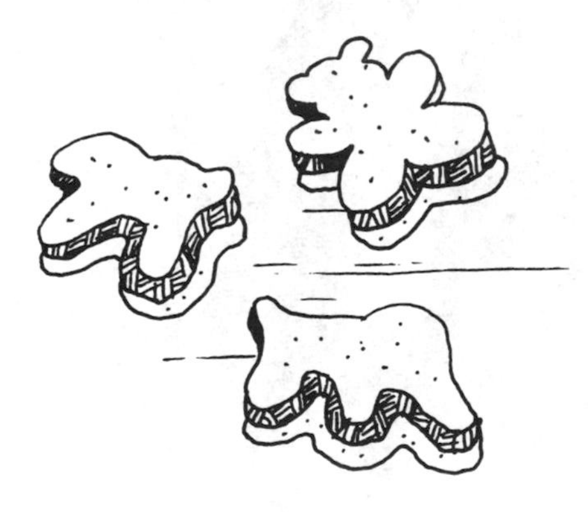

Bitsy Bread

1 package refrigerator biscuits
⅓ cup honey
½ cup coconut

Preheat............oven to 400 degrees.
Cut..................each biscuit into three pieces.
Roll..................each piece into a small ball.
Dip..................balls in honey.
Roll..................in coconut.
Place...............3 balls in each muffin cup in muffin pan.
Bake................at 400 degrees for 20 minutes.
Yield...............4 servings.

Breadsticks

1 package refrigerator biscuits
¼ cup butter, melted
Sesame seed

Preheat .... oven to 400 degrees.
Shape .... biscuits into 6 to 8-inch long sticks.
Pour .... half the butter into 9 x 12-inch baking pan; place sticks in butter.
Pour .... remaining butter over sticks.
Sprinkle .... with sesame seed.
Bake .... at 400 degrees for 10 minutes.

Crazy Quilt Bread

½ cup sugar
1 egg
1¼ cups milk
3 cups biscuit mix
½ cup mixed candied fruits
¾ cup chopped pecans

Preheat............oven to 350 degrees.
Grease.............9 x 5 x 3-inch loaf pan.
Combine...........sugar, egg, milk and biscuit mix in large mixer bowl. Beat on High for 1 minute. Batter will be lumpy.
Stir...................in fruits and pecans. Pour into greased loaf pan.
Bake.................at 350 degrees for 45 minutes.
Remove............from pan. Cool.

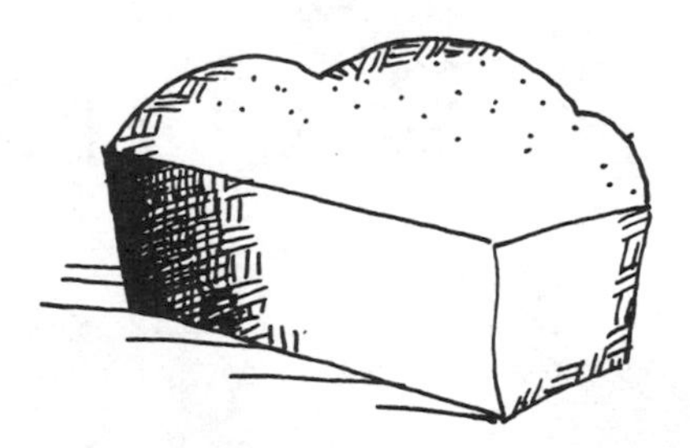

Crunchy Cheese Biscuits

½ cup margarine, softened
2 cups flour
2 cups grated cheese
2 cups rice cereal

Preheat............oven to 375 degrees.
Grease.............cookie sheet.
Combine...........all ingredients; mix well.
Shape..............into small balls, using hands. Flatten biscuits. Place on greased cookie sheet.
Bake................at 375 degrees for 8 to 10 minutes.
Yield...............40 biscuits.

Egyptian Palace Bread

4 slices white bread
1 cup honey

Preheat............oven to 300 degrees.
Cut..................crusts from bread.
Soak................bread in honey for 30 minutes.
Place...............in baking dish.
Bake................at 300 degrees for 25 minutes. Cool. May be served with cream to pour over bread.
Yield...............2 servings.

French Onion Bread

1 loaf French bread
¼ package dry onion soup mix
½ cup butter or margarine, softened

Preheat............oven to 400 degrees.
Cut..................loaf lengthwise.
Combine...........dry onion soup mix and butter. Spread on loaf.
Wrap................loaf in aluminum foil.
Bake.................at 400 degrees for 20 minutes.

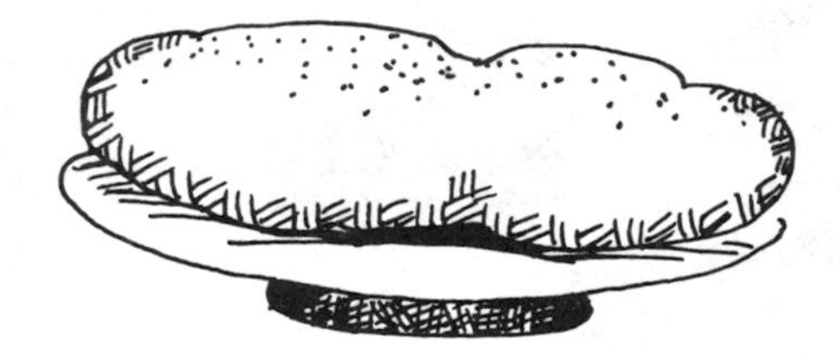

French Toast

1 egg
⅓ cup milk
1 teaspoon butter
4 slices bread

Beat .... egg until frothy.
Add .... milk; beat well.
Melt .... butter in skillet on Low heat.
Dip .... bread slices, one at a time, into egg mixture. Lift them into skillet with pancake turner.
Brown .... on each side.
Serve .... with confectioners' sugar, maple syrup or cinnamon and sugar, if desired.

Happy Apple Biscuits

1 cup crushed Wheat Chex
½ cup grated unpeeled apples
½ cup apple juice
2 cups biscuit mix
Pinch of nutmeg
Pinch of cinnamon

Preheat............oven to 450 degrees.
Combine........... Wheat Chex crumbs and apples; mix well. Pour apple juice over crumb mixture.
Combine...........biscuit mix, nutmeg and cinnamon; mix well. Stir into crumb mixture; mix well.
Drop................by spoonfuls onto buttered baking sheet.
Bake................at 450 degrees for 10 minutes.
Yield................16-18 servings.

Muffins In A Hurry

2 cups self-rising flour
1 cup milk
¼ cup salad dressing

Preheat............oven to 400 degrees.
Grease.............muffin pan.
Sift..................flour in mixing bowl.
Add.................milk and salad dressing; stir quickly until flour is just moistened and batter has lumpy appearance.
Fill...................greased muffin cups ⅔ full.
Bake................at 400 degrees for 20 minutes or until done.
Yield...............12 servings.

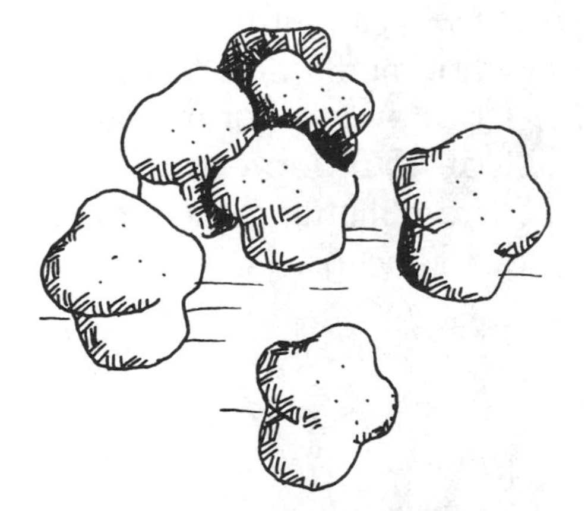

Popovers

1 cup flour
Pinch of salt
3 eggs
1 cup milk
1 teaspoon shortening

Preheat............oven to 450 degrees.
Combine...........flour and salt.
Break...............eggs into mixer bowl. Be careful not to get egg shells in eggs.
Beat................eggs well.
Add.................milk.
Add.................egg mixture slowly to flour, stirring. Beat for 2 minutes.
Place...............muffin pan in oven just for a short time to heat muffin pan. Be careful taking hot muffin pan from oven.
Pour................batter into hot muffin cups.
Bake................at 450 degrees for 30 minutes.
Remove............from muffin cups immediately.
Yield................8 servings.

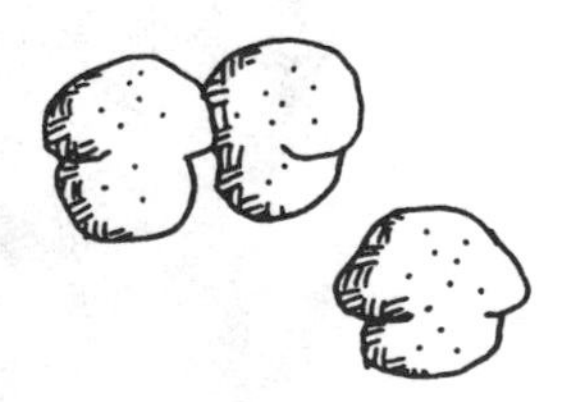

Southern Biscuits

1 can refrigerator biscuits
Cornmeal

Preheat............oven to 475 degrees.
Roll...................biscuits in cornmeal.
Bake..................at 475 degrees for 10 minutes.
Yield.................4 servings.

Spoon Bread

1 cup cornmeal
½ teaspoon salt
2 cups boiling water
2 tablespoons margarine
4 eggs, beaten
1 cup cold milk

Preheat............oven to 450 degrees.
Combine...........cornmeal, salt and 2 cups boiling water in saucepan. Stir for 1 minute. Remove from heat.
Add.................margarine; beat well.
Add.................eggs and cold milk; beat well.
Pour................into buttered baking dish.
Bake................at 450 degrees for 25 minutes. Serve in baking dish.
Yield...............8 servings.

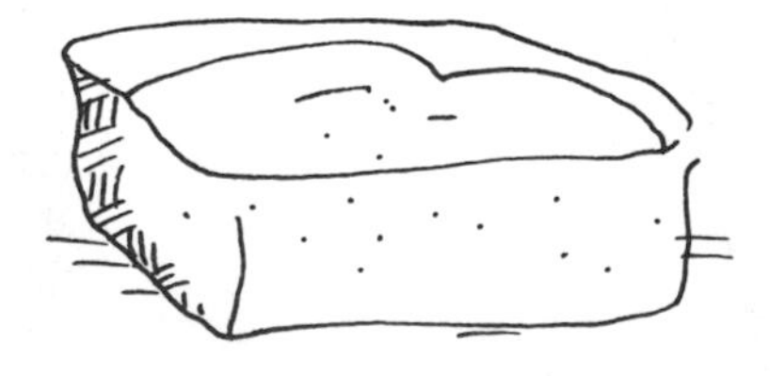

Desserts

All-American Sundae

1 large scoop raspberry sherbet
1 large scoop vanilla ice cream
½ cup blueberries
2 tablespoons whipped cream
1 maraschino cherry

Place ....sherbet in tall glass or sundae dish.
Add ....vanilla ice cream.
Top ....with blueberries.
Add ....whipped cream.
Place ....cherry on top.

Angels on Horseback

4 small milk chocolate bars
8 large graham crackers
12 marshmallows

Place ....chocolate bars on 4 graham crackers.
Place ....on cookie sheet. Turn oven setting to Broil. Broil until chocolate bars are slightly melted. Remove from oven.
Add ....3 marshmallows to each cracker.
Return ....to oven and broil until marshmallows are slightly brown. Remove from oven.
Cover ....with remaining 4 graham crackers.
Yield ....4 servings.

Apple Cloud

1 can apple pie filling
½ package white cake mix
1 stick margarine

Preheat ....oven to 350 degrees.
Grease ....8 x 8-inch baking dish.
Place ....pie filling in greased baking dish.
Sprinkle ....cake mix evenly over top.
Slice ....margarine into thin pats. Place pats over cake mix.
Bake ....at 350 degrees for 40 minutes. May be served plain or warm with ice cream.
Yield ....5-6 servings.

Apricot Nectar Delight

1 package marshmallows
1 12-ounce can apricot nectar
1 cup whipped cream
2 baked pie shells

Place ....marshmallows and apricot nectar in small saucepan. Heat on Low until marshmallows are melted.
Cool thoroughly.
Stir ....in whipped cream.
Pour ....into pie shells.
Place ....in freezer for 1 hour and 30 minutes or until set.

Cherry Cake

2 cans cherry pie filling
1 package white cake mix
½ cup chopped pecans
½ cup coconut
½ cup margarine

Preheat ....oven to 350 degrees.
Pour ....cherry pie filling in baking pan; spread evenly.
Pour ....cake mix over filling. DO NOT STIR.
Add ....pecans and coconut.
Place ....margarine in small saucepan. Heat on Low until margarine is melted; pour over top.
Bake ....at 350 degrees for 30 minutes or until browned.
Yield ....12 servings.

Cherry-Cheese Delight

1 3-ounce package cream cheese, softened
1 pint sour cream
1 can cherry pie filling

Combine ....cream cheese and sour cream.
Place ....layers of cream cheese mixture and cherry pie filling in sherbet glasses.
Refrigerate ....for at least 1 hour.
Yield ....6-8 servings.

Chinese Chewies

1 6-ounce package butterscotch pieces
½ cup peanut butter
1 3-ounce can chow mein noodles
1 cup miniature marshmallows

Place ....butterscotch pieces and peanut butter in medium saucepan.
Cook ....on Low for 6 minutes or until melted. Remove from heat.
Add ....noodles and marshmallows; stir well.
Line ....bottom of baking pan with waxed paper.
Drop ....1 teaspoon of mixture at a time onto waxed paper. Let stand until firm.
Yield ....35 servings.

Coconut Balls

1 package vanilla wafers
½ package miniature marshmallows
1 cup chopped English walnuts
1 can sweetened condensed milk
1 cup coconut

Place .... vanilla wafers in small plastic bag. Tie top of bag. Crush wafers.
Place .... vanilla wafer crumbs in large mixing bowl.
Add .... marshmallows, walnuts and milk; mix well.
Form .... into small balls.
Roll .... in coconut.
Yield .... 4 dozen.

Corn Flake Macaroons

Margarine
1 egg white
¼ cup sugar
Pinch of salt
½ teaspoon vanilla extract
⅓ cup corn flakes

Preheat ....oven to 350 degrees.
Grease ....cookie sheet with margarine.
Beat ....egg white until stiff peaks form, adding sugar gradually. Beat until mixture holds shape. Add salt and vanilla; beat well.
Fold ....in corn flakes.
Drop ....by teaspoonfuls onto greased cookie sheet.
Bake ....at 350 degrees for 20 to 25 minutes.

Fruit Cocktail Crumble

2 1-pound 13-ounce cans fruit cocktail
1 package yellow cake mix
2 sticks margarine

Preheat ....oven to 350 degrees.
Arrange ....fruit cocktail in 13 x 9 x 2-inch baking pan.
Sprinkle ....dry cake mix over fruit.
Slice ....margarine into thin pats. Place pats over cake mix.
Bake ....at 350 degrees for 40 minutes or until top is browned. Serve warm with a scoop of ice cream, sour cream or whipped cream, if desired.
Yield ....10-12 servings.

Fruit Sherbet

6 8-ounce orange drinks
1 8¼-ounce can crushed pineapple
1 14-ounce can condensed milk
1 6-ounce can frozen orange juice, thawed

Combine ....all ingredients; mix well.
Pour ....into ice trays with dividers removed.
Refrigerate ....stirring every 10 minutes to prevent the mixture separating.

Fun Fudge

1 3-ounce package cream cheese, softened
1 teaspoon vanilla extract
Pinch of salt
2 cups confectioners' sugar
½ cup chopped pecans

Grease ....9-inch pan.
Combine ....cream cheese, vanilla and salt in mixer bowl. Beat until creamy and smooth.
Add ....confectioners' sugar gradually, beating after each addition.
Stir ....in pecans.
Spread ....evenly in greased pan.
Refrigerate ....until firm.
Cut ....into squares.

Gooey Bars

1 package yellow cake mix
2 eggs
1 stick margarine, softened
1 package confectioners' sugar
1 8-ounce package cream cheese, softened
1 teaspoon vanilla extract

Preheat ....oven to 350 degrees.
Grease ....9 x 13-inch baking pan.
Combine ....yellow cake mix, eggs and margarine in mixer bowl; mix well. Press, using your hands, into greased baking pan.
Combine ....confectioners' sugar, cream cheese and vanilla in mixer bowl. Beat until creamy and smooth.
Spread ....over cake mixture.
Bake ....at 350 degrees for 35 minutes.
Cut ....into squares.

Graham Cracker Crust

1 tablespoon margarine
½ cup graham cracker crumbs
¼ teaspoon cinnamon

Preheat ....oven to 375 degrees.
Grease ....side and bottom of 9-inch pie plate using most of margarine for side.
Combine ....graham cracker crumbs and cinnamon; mix well. Press crumb mixture into pie plate, leaving bottom center thin.
Bake ....at 375 degrees for 5 minutes. Cool.

Grand Grapefruit

1 grapefruit
Margarine
1 tablespoon sugar
¼ teaspoon cinnamon

Cut .... grapefruit in half. Loosen fruit from skin. Cut each section close to the skin. Remove core.
Dot .... each half with margarine.
Combine .... sugar and cinnamon in bowl.
Sprinkle .... a small amount of sugar and cinnamon mixture over the grapefruit halves.
Place .... on broiler rack 4 inches from heat.
Broil .... for 8 minutes.

Hello Dolly Bars

1 stick margarine
1 cup graham cracker crumbs
1 cup flaked coconut
1 cup semisweet chocolate pieces
1 cup chopped pecans
1 15-ounce can sweetened condensed milk

Preheat ....oven to 350 degrees.
Place ....margarine in 9-inch square baking pan. Place in oven long enough to melt margarine. Be careful removing hot pan from oven.
Place ....graham cracker crumbs over margarine. Cover with coconut. Add chocolate pieces as next layer. Cover with pecans.
Pour ....condensed milk over top. DO NOT STIR.
Bake ....at 350 degrees for 30 minutes. Remove from oven.
Cool ....in pan.
Cut ....into squares.

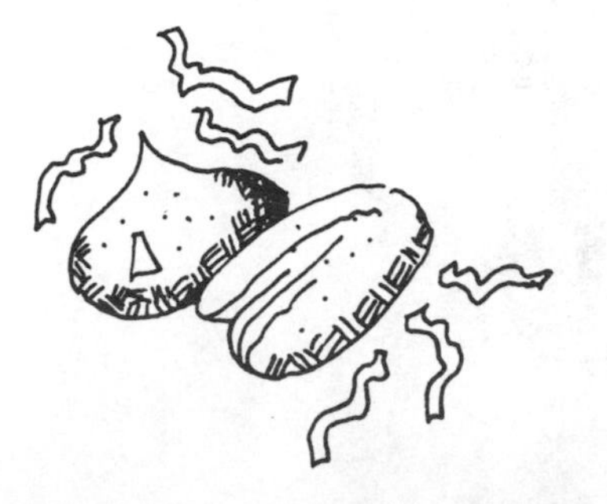

Kool-Aid Sherbet

1 cup sugar
1 package unsweetened Kool-Aid
3 cups milk

Dissolve ....sugar and Kool-Aid in milk. Pour into freezer tray. Freeze until mushy.
Spoon ....into mixer bowl; beat until smooth. Return to freezer tray.
Freeze ....for at least 2 hours.
Yield ....5-6 servings.

Lemon Delights

1 package lemon cake mix
1 4½-ounce carton Cool Whip
1 egg
Confectioners' sugar

Preheat ....oven to 350 degrees.
Combine ....lemon cake mix, Cool Whip and egg in large mixer bowl; mix well.
Form ....into small balls, using hands.
Roll ....in confectioners' sugar. Place on baking sheet.
Bake ....at 350 degrees for 8 minutes or until lightly browned.

Lemon Pie

1 15-ounce can sweetened condensed milk
1 6-ounce can frozen lemonade, thawed
1 small carton Cool Whip
1 9-inch graham cracker crust

Combine ....sweetened condensed milk and lemonade.
Add ....Cool Whip; stir slowly.
Pour ....into graham cracker crust
Refrigerate ....until serving time.

Microwave Brownies

2 cups graham cracker crumbs
1 6-ounce package semisweet chocolate pieces
½ cup chopped pecans
1⅓ cups sweetened condensed milk

NEVER ....PUT METAL OR ALUMINUM FOIL IN THE MICROWAVE OVEN.

Grease ....8-inch glass baking dish.
Combine ....graham cracker crumbs, chocolate pieces and pecans in greased baking dish; mix well.
Stir ....in sweetened condensed milk; spread evenly.
Microwave ....on High for 7 minutes. Let cool a few minutes in baking dish. Cut into squares.

Microwave Pudding Squares

2 cups milk
1 package vanilla pudding and pie filling mix
3 tablespoons margarine
1¼ cups graham cracker crumbs
¼ cup sugar
¼ cup peanut butter

NEVER.............. PUT METAL OR ALUMINUM FOIL IN THE MICROWAVE OVEN.

Combine........... milk and pudding mix in 4-cup glass measure.
Microwave........ on High for 5 to 6 minutes or until mixture boils, stirring occasionally during last half of cooking time. Set aside.
Place............... margarine in glass mixing bowl.
Microwave........ on High for 10 seconds.
Stir.................. in graham cracker crumbs, sugar and peanut butter; stir until crumbly.
Press................ ¾ of mixture into 1½-quart glass baking dish; spread evenly.
Top.................. with pudding mixture.
Sprinkle............ remaining graham cracker mixture over top.
Refrigerate........ for several hours.
Cut.................. into squares.

No-Crust Fudge Pie

2 squares unsweetened chocolate
½ cup margarine
2 eggs
1 cup sugar
2 tablespoons self-rising flour
1 teaspoon vanilla extract
½ cup pecan pieces

Place ....chocolate squares and margarine in medium saucepan. Heat over Low heat just until melted. Remove from heat.

Place ....eggs in small bowl; beat with a fork.

Add ....eggs, sugar, flour, vanilla and pecan pieces to chocolate mixture. Stir until completely mixed.

Grease ....a large pie pan with margarine.

Pour ....mixture into pie pan.

Place ....in cold oven. Turn oven setting to 350 degrees.

Bake ....for 30 minutes. Cool for 10 minutes before cutting.

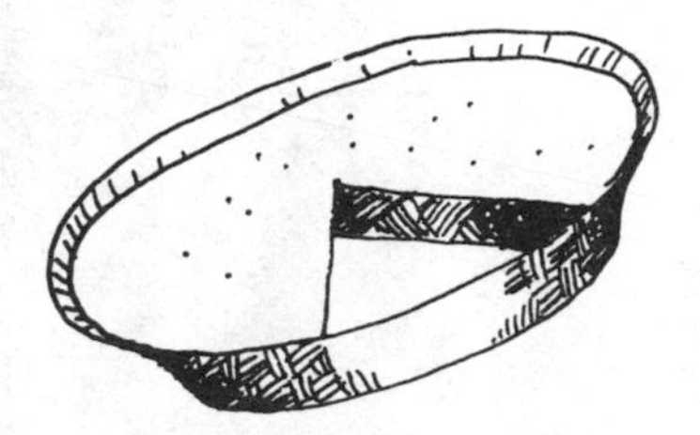

Oahu Frappe

½ cup sugar
¾ cup water
¾ cup orange juice
1½ cups unsweetened pineapple juice

Combine ....sugar and water in saucepan.
Cook ....over Medium heat for 5 minutes. Remove from heat. Cool slightly.
Add ....orange and pineapple juices; mix well. Pour into ice trays with dividers removed.
Freeze ....until mushy.
Serve ....in chilled glasses.
Yield ....6 servings.

Peachy Ginger

1 3-ounce package orange Jell-O
1 cup boiling water
1 cup ginger ale
1 cup diced canned peaches, drained

Dissolve ....Jell-O in boiling water in mixing bowl.
Add ....ginger ale. Place in refrigerator until it thickens but is not set.
Fold ....in peaches. Spoon into individual dishes.
Chill ....until firm.

Pecan Drops

1 package yellow cake mix
¼ cup margarine, softened
1 egg
⅓ cup milk
1 cup chopped pecans

Preheat ....oven to 375 degrees.
Combine ....cake mix, margarine, egg and milk in mixer bowl. Beat until light and fluffy.
Stir ....in pecans.
Drop ....by teaspoonfuls onto baking sheet.
Bake ....at 375 degrees until browned.
Yield ....5 dozen.

Peppermint Float

2 tablespoons finely crushed peppermint candy
1 quart peppermint ice cream
4 cups milk

Combine ....candy, 1 pint softened ice cream and milk in large mixer bowl. Beat at Low speed of electric mixer until slushy.
Pour ....into chilled glasses.
Top ....each with a scoop of remaining ice cream.

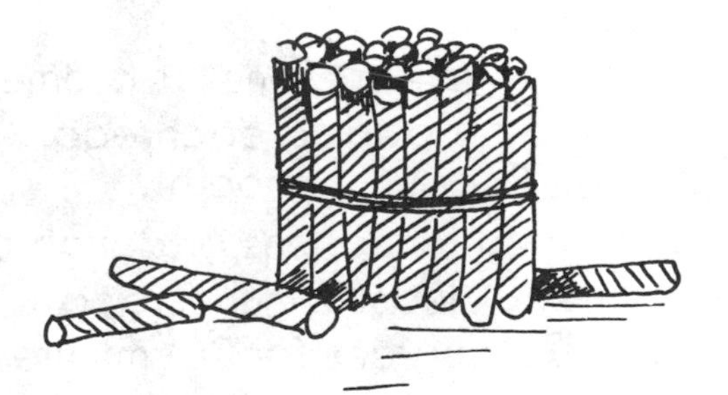

"What's Happening?" Fortune Cookies

¾ cup margarine, softened
2 cups sugar
1 teaspoon vanilla extract
3 eggs
1 cup sifted flour
40 small strips of paper with "fortunes"

Preheat ....oven to 375 degrees.
Grease ....cookie sheet and dust lightly with flour.
Place ....margarine and sugar in mixer bowl; beat until fluffy.
Add ....vanilla.
Add ....eggs to mixture, one at a time. Beat well after adding each egg.
Add ....flour. Beat until smooth.
Drop ....rounded teaspoons of dough on cookie sheet at least 2 inches apart.
Bake ....at 375 degrees for 20 minutes; remove from oven. Use a spatula to remove cookies from sheet.
Place ....a folded "fortune" on each cookie. Gently fold cookies in half. Pinch edges together and twist in the center.

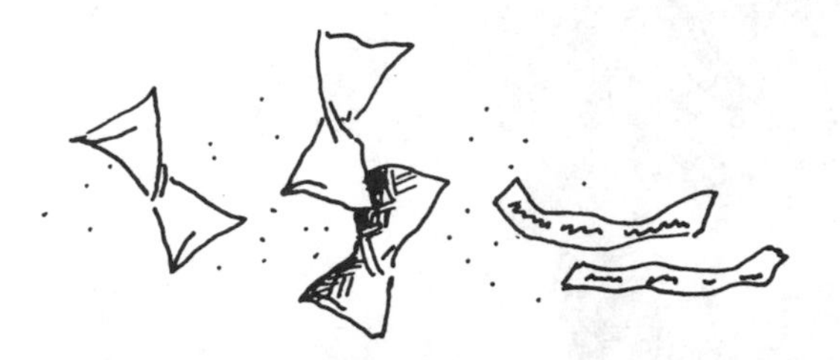

More Good Stuff

Alphabet Treats

½ cup light corn syrup
¼ cup sugar
1 3-ounce package Jell-O, any flavor
¾ cup salted peanuts
4 cups Alpha-Bits cereal

Combine ....syrup, sugar and Jell-O in saucepan. Stir over Low heat for 5 minutes or until sugar and Jell-O are completely dissolved.

Combine ....peanuts and cereal in large mixing bowl. Add Jell-O mixture; mix well.

Moisten ....hands in cold water. Form cereal mixture into 2-inch balls.

Wrap ....each in plastic wrap.

Boiled Eggs

Place ....eggs carefully in large saucepan. Add enough COLD water to cover the eggs.
Cook ....over Medium-high heat until water boils. Turn off heat.
Cover ....saucepan. Leave in pan for 15 minutes.
Cool ....eggs in cold water.
Crack ....shell and roll egg between hands. Start peeling at large end. Dip eggs in cold water to help remove shell. Make sure all shell is removed.

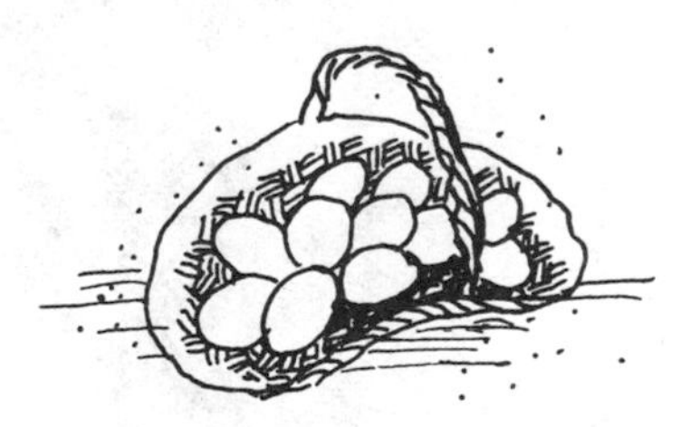

Cheese Dip

1 pound Velveeta cheese
½ can Ro-Tel tomatoes

Cut ....cheese into small pieces.
Place ....cheese in top of double boiler. Place top of double boiler in bottom of double boiler that has a small amount of water.
Cook ....slowly to melt cheese.
Add ....tomatoes slowly; heat thoroughly.
Serve ....as dip with large Fritos.

Cheese Dollars

1 pound Cheddar cheese, grated
7 tablespoons margarine
1 cup flour
½ teaspoon salt
¼ teaspoon red pepper
1 cup chopped pecans

Combine ....cheese, margarine, flour, salt and pepper in large mixing bowl. Mix well to form dough.
Add ....pecans; mix well.
Place ....dough on waxed paper. Shape dough into a roll. Place in refrigerator overnight.
Slice ....dough into thin circles.
Place ....on greased cookie sheet.
Bake ....at 325 degrees for 10 minutes.

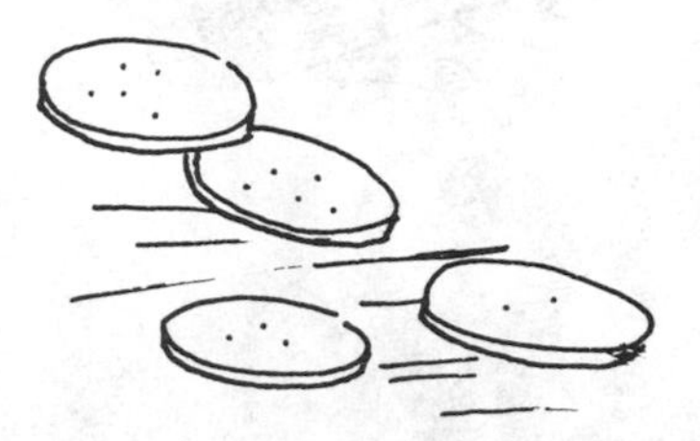

Microwave Hot Dogs

2 wieners
2 hot dog buns

NEVER ....PUT METAL OR ALUMINUM FOIL IN THE MICROWAVE OVEN.

Place ....wieners in split hot dog buns. Wrap loosely in paper napkin or paper towel. Place in microwave oven.

Microwave ....on High for 45 seconds.

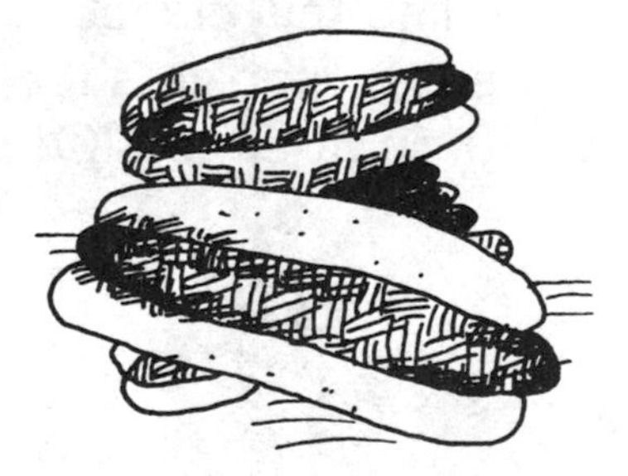

Puffs

Saltine crackers
Peanut butter
Marshmallows
Margarine

Spread ....several crackers with peanut butter. Place on cookie sheet.
Place ....marshmallow on top of each peanut butter cracker.
Place ....a small dot of margarine on each marshmallow.
Place ....in oven. Turn oven setting to Broil.
Broil ....until marshmallows are puffy and lightly browned. It doesn't take long.
Remove ....from oven; allow to cool.

Scrambled Eggs

6 eggs
¼ cup milk
¼ teaspoon salt
¼ teaspoon pepper
3 tablespoons margarine

Break .... eggs into small mixing bowl, being careful not to get any egg shell in the eggs.
Add .... milk, salt and pepper.
Beat .... egg mixture with fork.
Place .... margarine in skillet; heat over Medium heat until margarine is melted.
Pour .... egg mixture into skillet. Scramble with fork or spatula until eggs look fairly dry.

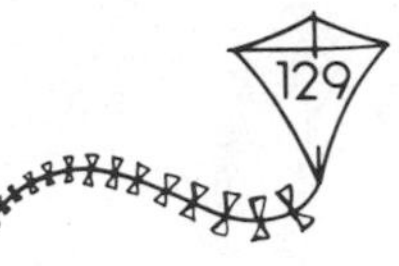

Pizza Bunny

3 cups cooked rice
2 eggs, beaten
1½ cups grated Cheddar cheese
1 10¾-ounce can pizza sauce
Pepperoni
Green olives
Black olives
Cheese
Pimento strips
Parsley

Pizza Bunny Crust–Combine rice, eggs and 1 cup Cheddar cheese. Spoon onto greased 17 x 14-inch baking sheet. Pat into bunny shape, moistening hands to prevent sticking. Bake at 450 degrees 15 minutes.

Pizza Bunny Topping–Spoon pizza sauce over crust; spread evenly. Sprinkle with ½ cup Cheddar cheese.

Pizza Bunny Decorations–Cut 4 slices pepperoni for buttons; cut 2 strips pepperoni for belt. Cut green olive in half lengthwise for eyes. Cut bottom from olive for nose. Make mouth from a wedge of black olive. Cut squares of cheese for belt buckle; surround with pimento strips. Bake at 450 degrees 10 to 15 minutes longer or until sauce is bubbly and cheese is melted. Let stand for 3 minutes. Remove to serving tray.

The Final Touch–Garnish with parsley stems for whiskers. Fill a small basket with parsley and candy eggs.

Photograph for this recipe on page 1.

Animal Cut-Out Sandwiches

4 hard-cooked eggs, chopped
⅓ cup sour cream
¼ cup finely chopped sweet pickle
2 teaspoons grated onion
1 teaspoon prepared mustard
½ teaspoon salt
Bread
Butter, softened
American cheese slices

Combine eggs, sour cream, pickle, onion, mustard and salt; blend well. Cut bread into animal shapes, using cookie cutters. Butter bread animals. Spread 1 bread animal with about 1 tablespoon egg mixture; top with matching bread animal. Butter tops lightly. Cut cheese slices with cookie cutters to match bread animals; place on matching animal sandwich.

Photograph for this recipe on page 2.

Painted Daisy Cookies

1½ cups flour
¼ teaspoon each baking powder, soda and nutmeg
½ cup butter
1 egg
Sugar
½ teaspoon vanilla extract
½ teaspoon grated lemon peel
1 egg yolk
Food color
Semisweet chocolate pieces

Combine flour, baking powder, soda and nutmeg. Cut in butter until mixture resembles coarse crumbs. Beat egg; add ½ cup sugar gradually, beating well. Stir in vanilla and lemon peel. Blend egg mixture into flour mixture, beating to form dough. Cover and chill. Roll out dough on lightly floured surface to ¼-inch thickness. Cut out cookies with a floured 3½-inch round cookie cutter. Place on lightly buttered cookie sheets. Bake at 375 degrees for 6 to 8 minutes. Cool. To decorate, lightly beat egg yolk; add ¼ teaspoon water. Divide egg mixture into custard cups; add desired food colors. Dip chocolate pieces in egg mixture; place in center of cookies. Paint on flower petals with small paint brushes; sprinkle with sugar. Yield: 18 large cookies.

Photograph for this recipe on page 2.

Purple Cow

1½ cups milk
3 tablespoons frozen grape juice concentrate, thawed
Vanilla ice cream

Place milk, grape juice concentrate and 2 scoops vanilla ice cream in blender container; blend until smooth. Pour into two 12-ounce glasses. Top with scoops of vanilla ice cream.

Photograph for this recipe on page 2.

Milk Party Punch

½ cup powdered red punch drink mix
5 cups cold milk
Milk ice cubes

Pour drink mix into bowl; stir in ½ cup cold water until dissolved. Pour 3 cups milk into serving pitcher. Pour dissolved punch into milk, stirring constantly. Pour 2 cups milk into ice cube tray; freeze until firm. Add milk ice cubes.

Photograph for this recipe on page 2.

Rice-A-Burgers

1 pound ground beef
2 eggs, slightly beaten
3 cups cooked rice
2 teaspoons seasoned salt
¾ cup catsup
½ teaspoon oregano
4 slices Cheddar cheese

Combine ground beef, eggs, rice and salt in large mixing bowl; mix well. Spread into 8 foil "pans" or 1 large pizza pan. (For foil pans, use 8-inch circles of aluminum foil, 3 layers each. Use coffee can lid or cardboard circle as guide for shaping. Crimp edges of foil as you would pie crust to give sturdy edge.) Spread with catsup; sprinkle with oregano. Bake at 450 degrees for 10 minutes. Top with cheese cut into small triangles. Bake at 450 degrees for 5 minutes longer or until cheese is bubbly. Yield: 8 servings.

Photograph for this recipe on page 35.

Lemon Tartar Sandwiches

1 8-ounce package frozen fried fish cakes
3 teaspoons lemon juice
½ cup mayonnaise
2 tablespoons finely chopped dill pickle
2 tablespoons finely chopped green onion
1 tablespoon chopped canned pimento
1 teaspoon grated lemon peel
4 hamburger buns, toasted
1 large tomato, sliced
Lettuce

Sprinkle fish cakes with 2 teaspoons lemon juice. Prepare according to package directions. Combine mayonnaise, dill pickle, onion, pimento, lemon peel and 1 teaspoon lemon juice. Spread on hamburger buns; layer with fish, tomato and lettuce. Yield: 4 servings.

Photograph for this recipe on page 36.

Tuna Sandwich By The Inch

2 7-ounce cans tuna, drained and flaked
½ cup mayonnaise
¼ cup chopped celery
2 tablespoons sweet pickle relish
Grated rind and juice of ½ lemon
1 loaf French bread
Lettuce
1 avocado, sliced
½ red onion, sliced
3 slices sharp cheese, cut diagonally

Combine tuna, mayonnaise, celery, relish, lemon rind and lemon juice in large mixing bowl; mix well. Cut French bread in half lengthwise; layer with tuna mixture, lettuce, avocado, onion and cheese. Garnish with stuffed olives and cucumber slices, if desired. Cut into thick slices. Yield: 6 servings.

Photograph for this recipe on page 36.

Fresh Broccoli With Mild Cheese Sauce

1 bunch broccoli
1 teaspoon salt
Pinch of pepper
2 tablespoons butter or margarine
2 tablespoons flour
1 cup milk
1 cup shredded American cheese

Rinse broccoli; remove large leaves and tough part of stalks. Separate into individual spears. Place in large saucepan with ½ inch boiling water. Add salt and pepper; cover. Simmer for 10 to 12 minutes or until tender crisp. Melt butter in a

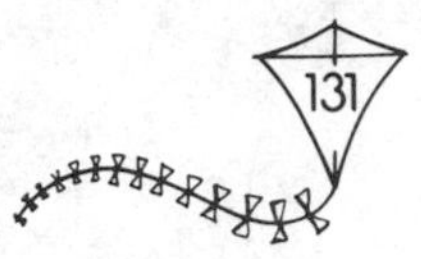

saucepan; blend in flour. Stir in milk, stirring constantly. Cook until sauce thickens and comes to a boil. Add cheese; cook until melted and blended, stirring. Drain broccoli; cover with cheese sauce. Yield: 4-6 servings.

Photograph for this recipe on page 69.

Confetti Coleslaw

4 cups shredded cabbage
½ cup shredded pared carrot
1 teaspoon salt
1 teaspoon sugar
½ cup mayonnaise
1 tablespoon vinegar
1 tablespoon milk
1 small red apple, chopped

Combine cabbage and carrot; sprinkle with salt and sugar. Combine mayonnaise, vinegar and milk; mix well. Add to cabbage mixture; mix well. Chill. Add apple just before serving. Yield: 8 servings.

Photograph for this recipe on page 69.

Backyard Coney

½ pound ground beef
¼ cup chopped onion
1 6-ounce can tomato paste
¾ teaspoon salt
¼ teaspoon garlic salt
¼ teaspoon chili powder
Pinch of oregano
¾ cup drained kidney beans
1 loaf French bread, split lengthwise
1¼ cups shredded lettuce
4 wieners, heated, split lengthwise
8 Cheddar cheese triangles

Brown ground beef and onion; drain. Add tomato paste, ⅔ cup water and seasonings; cover. Simmer for 20 minutes. Add kidney beans. Simmer 10 minutes longer. Spoon hot mixture on bottom half of bread loaf. Top with lettuce, wieners, cheese and top half of bread loaf. Secure sandwich with toothpicks. Cut into 8 servings.

Photograph for this recipe on page 70.

Carrousel Cutouts

½ cup butter, softened
½ cup sugar
1 egg, slightly beaten
⅓ cup molasses
1 tablespoon vinegar
2¼ cups flour
¾ teaspoon soda
1 teaspoon ginger
½ teaspoon cinnamon
½ teaspoon ground cloves
¼ teaspoon salt
1½ cups confectioners' sugar
½ teaspoon vanilla extract
2½ to 3 tablespoons milk

Combine butter and sugar; cream until light and fluffy. Add egg, molasses and vinegar; mix well. Sift together next 6 ingredients. Add gradually to creamed mixture, mixing well after each addition. Chill. Roll dough on lightly floured surface to ¼-inch thickness. Cut with assorted large cookie cutters. Place on ungreased cookie sheets. Bake at 375 degrees for 7 to 9 minutes; cool. Combine confectioners' sugar, vanilla and milk; mix well. Glaze cookies; allow to dry thoroughly. Paint with food colors, as desired. Yield: 3-4 dozen.

Photograph for this recipe on page 70.

Dip and Crunch

1 3-ounce package cream cheese, softened
½ cup mayonnaise
3 tablespoons catsup
Carrots, pared and cut in diagonal slices
Lettuce, cut in chunks
Cauliflowerets
Cherry tomatoes
Celery pieces

Combine cream cheese, mayonnaise and catsup; mix well. Serve as dip with vegetables. Yield: 1 cup dip.

Photograph for this recipe on page 69.

Spring Bonnet Cake

1 package yellow cake mix
1 cup water
Florida orange juice
1 tablespoon grated orange rind
2 eggs
2 egg whites
1½ cups sugar
Pinch of salt
½ teaspoon cream of tartar
1 teaspoon vanilla extract
4 drops of yellow food coloring
Small colored gumdrops
Large colored gumdrops
1 cup Florida orange sections

Combine cake mix, water, ⅓ cup orange juice, orange rind and 2 eggs in large bowl; blend until moistened. Beat according to cake mix package directions. Pour half the batter into greased and floured 8-inch round cake pan. Pour remaining batter into greased and floured 1½-quart ovenproof bowl. Bake the 8-inch layer at 350 degrees for 30 to 35 minutes. Bake the bowl cake at 350 degrees for 40 to 45 minutes. Cool for 10 minutes; remove from pan and bowl. Cool on rack. Combine egg whites, sugar, salt, cream of tartar and ½ cup orange juice in top of double boiler; beat well. Place over boiling water; beat constantly at High speed of electric mixer for 7 minutes or until stiff peaks form. Add vanilla and coloring; beat 1 minute longer. Invert 8-inch layer on plate; frost side and top. Cut a thin slice from top of bowl cake to make it level. Invert bowl cake on frosted layer. Frost generously; round top to form bonnet. Slice small gumdrops; place around base to make hat band. Cut large gumdrops into 4 sections with scissors, being careful not to cut all the way through. Cut small gumdrops into 3 sections. Separate sections by pinching to resemble flower petals. Cut green gumdrops to make stems. Decorate top and side of bonnet with gumdrop flowers and stems. Place orange sections around base.

Photograph for this recipe on page 103.

Pumpkin Cake

3¼ cups sifted flour
Sugar
2 teaspoons soda
1½ teaspoons salt
¼ teaspoon baking powder
1 teaspoon cinnamon
½ teaspoon ground cloves
¾ teaspoon nutmeg
¾ cup shortening
Frozen Florida orange juice, thawed
6 tablespoons water
1 15-ounce can applesauce
3 eggs
1½ cups raisins
1 cup chopped nuts
2 egg whites
½ teaspoon cream of tartar
1 teaspoon vanilla extract
Food coloring
½ small banana

Sift together flour, 2¼ cups sugar, soda, salt, baking powder and spices in large mixer bowl. Add shortening, 6 tablespoons orange juice, water and applesauce; beat 2 minutes at Medium speed. Add eggs; beat 2 minutes longer. Blend in raisins and nuts. Pour into greased and floured 10-inch tube pan. Bake at 350 degrees for 1 hour and 15 to 20 minutes or until cake tests done. Cool in pan for 15 to 20 minutes. Remove from pan; cool completely. Combine egg whites, 1½ cups sugar, cream of tartar, ½ cup orange juice and vanilla in top of double boiler, over boiling water. Beat with electric mixer at High speed for 5 to 7 minutes or until peaks form. Place ½ cup frosting in small bowl; tint with green food coloring. Tint remaining frosting orange, using several drops of yellow food coloring and 1 or 2 drops red. Round top by cutting off small amount of cake all the way around. Place cake on plate. Stand banana in center of cake to form stem. Frost cake with orange frosting. Frost stem with green frosting.

Photograph for this recipe on page 104.

Bob-For-Orange Punch

5 Florida oranges
Whole cloves
1 cup sugar
1 cup water
2 2-inch sticks cinnamon
3 quarts Florida orange juice
1 quart apple juice

Stud oranges with whole cloves; place in baking dish. Bake at 325 degrees for 3 hours. Combine sugar, water, 12 whole cloves and cinnamon in saucepan. Simmer 10 minutes. Remove cloves and cinnamon. Add juices; heat. Pour into heatproof punch bowl. Float baked oranges on punch.

Photograph for this recipe on page 104.

INDEX

SNACKS

MEATS

SALADS

VEGETABLES

COLOR PHOTOGRAPH RECIPES

Photography Credits

Cover and Illustrations: Designer–Lee Hamblen; Rice Council; United Dairy Industry Association; Sunkist Growers Inc.; United Fresh Fruit and Vegetable Association; Florida Department of Citrus.